Philip Roth through the Lens of Kepesh

Philip Roth through the Lens of Kepesh

Paul McDonald and Samantha Roden

𝓗𝓔𝓑 ☼ HUMANITIES-EBOOKS, LLP

The Authors have asserted their right to be identified as the authors of this Work in accordance with the Copyright, Designs and Patents Act 1988.

First published by *Humanities-Ebooks, LLP,*
Tirril Hall, Tirril, Penrith CA10 2JE

The PDF and ePub versions are available to private purchasers outside the UK & EU exclusively from http://www.humanities-ebooks.co.uk and to readers in the UK and EU from Google Play.

The PDF is available to libraries from EBL/Ebrary and EBSCO

The paperback is available at a discount from Lulu.com

ISBN 978-1-84760-363-0 Pdf Ebook
ISBN 978-1-84760-364-7 Paperback
ISBN 978-1-84760-365-4 Kindle
ISBN 978-1-84760-366-1 ePub

For Miss Whizzington

Contents

General Editors' Introduction

Approaches to Contemporary American Literature

The election of Barack Obama as 44th President of the United States in November 2008 represented both an historic and a symbolic moment in the history of the nation. Not only was Obama the first non-white President; he was also a figure whose origins lay at the edge of, and beyond, the geographical boundaries of the country. Born in Hawaii—the newest state and one far removed from continental North America—Obama came from a region unfamiliar to most Americans, unless they had spent vacations there; the son of a Kenyan father and white American mother, he was a reminder of America's origins as a nation of immigrants, but also an anomaly in a country where the overwhelming majority of African Americans are descendants of slaves. Moreover, Obama spent four years of his childhood in Jakarta, Indonesia, experiencing a life very different from the norms of the United States.

In other ways, however, Obama's biography enacted a familiar myth: the rise from a 'broken' home with an absent father, success in high school (interrupted by moments of crisis featuring alcohol and illicit drug use), through an education at Columbia and then Harvard Law School, to triumph in local Chicago politics and finally the Presidency epitomised the myth—if not the actuality—of the American Dream. While the road to the White House has been tougher for some than for others, with Abraham Lincoln and Bill Clinton possibly coming closest to being antecedents of Obama's path, even the scions of wealthy, well connected families, such as George and George W. Bush, have always highlighted their populist roots in their political campaigns.

Of course, Obama's election by no means signified the end of racism in America: jails remain disproportionately occupied by

African American males, economic inequalities continue to be marked along ethnic lines and even as distinguished an African American as Harvard professor Henry Louis Gates, Jr. was, in 2009, a victim of arrest apparently based on racial profiling as he attempted to enter his own home. And yet, in the past thirty or forty years, there have been a series of pronounced shifts in academic approaches to racial, ethnic and gender issues, that have called attention to the multitudinous voices constituting what Walt Whitman famously called a 'teeming nation of nations'.

For present purposes, our focus will remain on the literature and literary criticism of the period running from, roughly, the early 1970s to the present. Until then, the literary canon had been constructed around a body of white, largely male, New Yorkers and New Englanders, most notably the figures of F.O. Matthiessen's *American Renaissance* (1941) and Henry James ('The Master'). In the Twentieth Century the scope widened to include mid-Westerners such as F. Scott Fitzgerald and Ernest Hemingway, and, post-World War Two, Jewish American novelists including Saul Bellow, E. L. Doctorow and Philip Roth, who were placed alongside perpetuators of a more 'traditional' American literature such as John Updike, and the new voices of what would eventually be labelled 'postmodernism', such as Thomas Pynchon and, slightly later, Don DeLillo. While there is no doubt that Nineteenth Century writers—most notably, Whitman, Herman Melville and Mark Twain—had recognised the multicultural possibilities of America, it is the era we are concerned with in this series that changed the way the country viewed and narrated itself in literature, with multicultural fictions that often combined critical and commercial success. Doctorow's *Ragtime* (1975) famously interweaves the stories of three families to rewrite the history and parody the mythology of the United States. The opening pages of the novel rapidly move from a turn-of-the-century world that seems straight out of Henry James or Edith Wharton to a sudden realization of the plurality of American life:

> That was the style, that was the way people lived. Women were stouter then. They visited the fleet carrying white parasols. Everyone wore white in summer. Tennis racquets were hefty and

the racquet faces elliptical. There was a lot of sexual fainting. There were no Negroes. There were no immigrants.

…

In New York City the papers were full of the shooting of the famous architect Stanford White by Harry K. Thaw, eccentric scion of a coke and railroad fortune. Harry K. Thaw was the husband of Evelyn Nesbit, the celebrated beauty who had once been Stanford White's mistress. The shooting took place in the roof garden of the Madison Square Garden on 26th Street, a spectacular block-long building of yellow brick and terra cotta that White himself had designed in the Sevillian style. It was the opening night of a revue entitled Mamzelle Champagne, and as the chorus sang and danced the eccentric scion wearing on this summer night a straw boater and heavy black coat pulled out a pistol and shot the famous architect three times in the head. On the roof. There were screams. Evelyn fainted. She had been a well-known artist's model at the age of fifteen. Her underclothes were white. Her husband habitually whipped her. She happened once to meet Emma Goldman, the revolutionary. Goldman lashed her with her tongue. Apparently there were Negroes. There were immigrants.

E. L. Doctorow, *Ragtime* (1975)

Among the many strengths of Doctorow's novel is its ability to highlight the way that an intermingling of disparate voices—immigrant, African American and 'white'—is at the heart of American creativity, whilst the book provides constant reminders both of the power of national mythologies such as Benjamin Franklin's rags to riches narrative, and of just how hard it is to sustain principled opposition to this narrative in the face of the financial inducements and social opportunities offered to a few individuals. The transformation of the East European immigrant Tateh, defined by his socialism, devotion to his family and to apparently unshakable faith in core moral values into the Baron Ashkenazy, creator of movies depicting an implausibly harmonious (and immensely popular) multi-ethnic gang of American children finally reiterates Doctorow's insistence that history has always been told by the masters, but also his belief that—by 1975—there was the possibility of other histories emerging.

At least within the academic community, Doctorow was probably correct: while studies of Hawthorne, Melville and James most certainly did not disappear, they were joined by a growing corpus of studies that insisted that yes, 'there *were* Negroes [or 'African Americans']. There *were* immigrants.' Studies such as Jane Tompkins's *Sensational Designs* (1986), Michael J. Denning's *Mechanic Accents* (1987) and Russell J. Reising's *The Unusable Past* (1987) assimilated and developed the work of earlier multicultural critics such as Annette Kolodny and Richard Slotkin to challenge the assertions underpinning the construction of the American canon and demand spaces for works by women novelists and the writings of African Americans and immigrants. And while the *literary* value of literature did at times seem to disappear from the interminable canon wars of the 1980s and 1990s (though not in the books cited above), the theoretical battles that quite often really did split departments into highly antagonistic factions in the late-Twentieth Century do seem to have resulted in a Twenty-First Century critical culture in which a return to stress on the literariness of literature lives alongside the general embrace of the fact that writing the canon is not the preserve of Ivy League white males.

At the same time as the work of critics such as Tompkins and Reising recovered the long-marginalised presence of writings by women and African Americans, new generations of American writers from a plentitude of ethnic and class positions have assumed pivotal places in contemporary American literature. While there seems to be no doubt that Toni Morrison is the best known—and one of the most highly acclaimed—of these voices, she is but one figure in a literary marketplace that increasingly problematises the notion of what American literature *is* and the kinds of critical tools required to discuss it in any meaningful fashion. The focus on the 'playful', experimental postmodernism of the 1960s and 1970s has been replaced by (or, at least, joined by) a return to the search for the *authentic* experience of narratives of migration (both to and from the United States), of the precarious balancing of assimilation to a dominant culture and the desire to retain a culture of one's own, and of the eternal questioning of what it means to be an 'American'.

In an increasingly 'globalised' community, these narratives are now as often recounted by writers from North Africa or China as by those from Eastern Europe, but most seem to retain a faith—at some level—in the mythological promises of the United States that seemed to have been brought to life by Barack Obama. To listen to the taxi drivers of Boston, or Austin, or San Francisco, or Denver is to hear life stories—if not quite *novels*—that are at once strikingly different in the details of war zones fled and disillusionment with the 'old' country, and an innate faith in the possibilities of a world still almost as new as that first viewed by Fitzgerald's Dutch sailors at the end of *The Great Gatsby*. And while contemporary American literature is as often marked by a disillusionment with the nation that can be traced through most of the nation's literary history, this is accompanied by the sense of possibility that is heard so often in the voices of 'ordinary' Americans, but also by the recognition that—post-9/11—the United States is as vulnerable to external forces as are the nations left behind.

The enormous diversity of American literatures currently being created ensures that a series called 'Approaches to Contemporary American Literature' is bound to be both eclectic and inconsistent. There is no longer even the possibility—or the desire—to create a master narrative able to 'contain' (to return once more to Whitman) the multitudinous voices that constitute a 'national' narrative. Indeed, recent approaches to the Trans- or Post-national condition would rightly question the enduring legitimacy of such a concept. This means that the series makes no claims to unfurl organically, beneath any but the broadest of themes. Books studying the emergence and development of particular hyphenated American groups are accompanied by those looking at genre, or at single authors. To study the world we live in requires tools and methodologies that may differ from those used to approach the texts of the past. What unites the books in this series is their contribution to our understanding of the here and now.

Introduction

In a career spanning well over half a century, the Jewish American novelist Philip Roth has told many different stories in many different ways. His work moves from traditional realism, through dark comedy, postmodernism, experimental-confession, to neo-realism, and, by the time Roth announced his retirement from writing in 2012, he'd covered a vast amount of ground as a storyteller. However, in some ways his preoccupations as a novelist have varied very little. From the first stories he published in the late 50s, through to his final novella, *Nemesis* (2011), Roth has focused on the conflict between duty and desire. This manifests itself in different ways for different protagonists, of course, but it is difficult to find a Roth story that doesn't have a version of this dilemma at its heart. In our view this is expressed most clearly via Roth's scholar-hero David Kepesh, and we offer a reading of Roth's oeuvre which aims to put the three novellas in which Kepesh appears at the centre. This does not mean that our focus will be entirely on Kepesh or the Kepesh books. We will offer a chronological reading of Roth's work, addressing the Kepesh novels in the context of his entire fictional output, but revealing as we do so the centrality of these stories and the significance they have in relation to Roth's philosophical and aesthetic preoccupations.

The Kepesh trilogy spans three decades of Roth's career, beginning with *The Breast* in 1972, continuing with the *Professor of Desire* in 1977 and concluding with *The Dying Animal* in 2001. The trilogy has received scant scholarly attention to date, with several book length studies treating it as a minor aside in Roth's oeuvre. Thus, David Brauner's *Philip Roth* (2007), virtually ignores all three books, and David Goodbar's *The Major Phases of Philip Roth* (2011), while discussing *Professor*, has little more than a paragraph on *The Breast*, and omits *Animal* altogether. This is strange given that, as one critic noted, 'Kepesh's style comes the closest among Roth's characters to matching the author's true voice as revealed in his various essays' (Kevin. R. West, 232), and several others have observed similarities between Kepesh's opinions and those of his creator.[1] It often feels that Kepesh is close to Roth, perhaps as much so as with his more obvious pseudo-autobiographical incarnations like Nathan Zuckerman, or 'Philip Roth.' We aim to show that these novellas are not only worthy of critical analysis in their own right, then, but also, as suggested, that an appreciation of Roth's themes and strategies in this trilogy can deepen our understanding of his entire fictional enterprise, offering an invaluable perspective on his work.

This book begins with a discussion of the desire versus restraint dilemma that informs all of the early stories, from those collected in *Goodbye Columbus* (1959), to the controversial *Portnoy's Complaint* (1969). This provides a context for a discussion of *The Breast* (1972), where the quintessential Rothian conflict is writ large. Viewed as a coda for *Portnoy*, Kepesh's metamorphosis becomes both a symptom of the fractured psyche and an expression of an overweening desire to unite it. In the starkest possible terms, it registers the desire/restraint, id/superego conflict that torments earlier heroes like Neil Klugman and Alex Portnoy; in one sense Kepesh's status as a breast becomes a comic expression of their dilemma. The joke that Roth plays on his protagonist here—i.e. transforming him into an ironic representation of his desires, and hence an unstable symbol of unity—is akin to several attempts in later works to construct images that symbolically encapsulate his characters' conflicts and hold them in transient symbolic stasis.

In his review of *The Breast*, Peter Fenninger suggested that the novella 'might be an exercise in introducing ideas for a longer work,' and with the publication of *The Professor of Desire* this turned out to be the case ('*The Breast* Needs More,' unpaginated). Here Roth continues a postmodern project that begins in *The Breast*, and continues in novels such as *My Life as a Man* (1974). Like the latter, *The Professor of Desire* makes self-conscious references to Roth's own

---

1   For instance, West cites Elaine Showalter's observation of the 'little distance between alter ego and the author,' and Carlin Romano's contention that it's 'the author talking' (232).

fiction (most notably *The Breast*), and employs overt intertextuality to destabilise its narrative; he creates a postmodern context for Kepesh's story and the psychodynamics of desire and restraint. In this book Kepesh is still searching for ways to reconcile the duelling aspects of his psyche, pulled as he is between the lifestyles of scholarship and indulgence. This is underscored by the ambiguous comic image of Kafka's whore. Kafka is often emblematic of self-denial in Roth's writing, and Kafka's whore becomes a polysemic symbol expressing both restraint and desire simultaneously. It is a repellent signifier representing a fundamentally irreconcilable conflict, and suggesting again that there can be no resolution to Kepesh's dilemma, except the one that befalls him in the earlier book—his transformation into a mammary gland.

It will be seen how these early incarnations of Kepesh anticipate the comic identities of later Roth heroes; for instance, like Kepesh, Roth's writer-hero, Nathen Zuckerman, is a performer in search of the role that will reconcile his fractured psyche. The *Zuckerman Bound* (1986) trilogy, together with novels such as *The Counterlife* (1987) see him shift between 'real' and imaginary personas, including pornographer, obstetrician, lover of Anne Frank, hero, saviour of Jewish cultural heritage, and, not least, author. These themes continue in the so-called 'Philip Roth' books where the author blurs the distinction between fact and fiction still further. As in the *Professor of Desire* these books destabilise narrative and apparently undermine the possibility of meaning, whilst at the same time registering a profound desire for coherence. *The Counterlife* also picks up on the notion of the pastoral explored in the closing sections of *Professor*. In the latter the farmhouse scenes with Kepesh's lover Claire seemingly represent a potential life of fulfilment for the hero, but this is undermined as his self-understanding deepens; *The Counterlife*—a novel which constructs England and Englishness as a metaphor for the pastoral ideal—continues to unpick the idea of a conflict-free life and expose its absurdity. Indeed, increasingly Roth's books stress the inevitability and even the desirability of conflict, and this, together with an acceptance of uncertainty, becomes central to his philosophy and his aesthetic. He addresses this in relation to character in *The Counterlife*, for instance, when he re-explores the notion of a performing-self first mooted in *Professor*. We will show that an acknowledgement of uncertainty begins in *The Breast* and then deepens through the books he produces in subsequent decades.

While uncertainty appears to be inevitable for Roth, the search for meaning is crucial and ennobling. This is seen in *The Breast* where Kepesh's struggle to interpret his predicament is nothing less than heroic. The human need to find meaning appears to be fundamental to Roth, and it features again in the 1993 novel, *Operation Shylock* where the theme of contradiction is re-recast as a doppelganger story. Here 'Roth' is the hero of his own fiction; he is shown to be struggling like Kepesh to live an ordered life, even as his other self—his doppelganger Pipik—disrupts it. The doppelganger theme once more represents both a desire for unity, and recognition of the inevitability of fragmentation.

Where *Professor* dramatizes a clash between the professor and the rake, Roth's 1995 masterpiece, *Sabbath's Theater*, appears to show the rake get the upper hand—unlike with Kepesh, Micky Sabbath's Super Ego appears never to be in abeyance, and dissent and self-indulgence dominate his philosophy of life. But even here the hero's behaviour seems to make a moral point, qualifying his 'immoral' conduct and constructing yet another contradiction reminiscent of the Kepesh stories.

When Nathan Zuckerman appears again in the so-called American Trilogy, it is to feature in novels that explore the possibility of a conflict-free life. Various utopian narratives appear to offer meaning and structure of the kind that Kepesh desires at the end of *Professor*, but once again none are viable; indeed, all are potentially pernicious. We address this theme at length in a discussion of the American Trilogy's final instalment, *The Human Stain*, where Puritanism and Political Correctness are seen as controlling narratives that encroach on the individual's desire for autonomy.

The prospect of individual autonomy is one of Roth's key themes throughout his career: time and again his novels ponder the possibility of self-determination. Roth's heroes are often seen struggling to free themselves from the defining narratives of heritage or convention:

these commitment issues feature as far back as *Goodbye Columbus* (1959) and *Letting Go*, and can be seen later in novels such as *Sabbath's Theater* where the hero's nonconformity takes an extreme form. In the third instalment of the Kepesh trilogy, *The Dying Animal*, this theme is re-examined more subtly. Here Kepesh is reintroduced as a seventy-year old man torn between his desire for his young lover Consuela, and his reluctance to commit to her. This final book in the trilogy also sheds fresh light on Roth's attitude to masculinity and what critics occasionally see as an unhealthy tendency to privilege the male perspective; according to some this is such a feature in Roth's writing that, as Carmen Callil remarked, it's 'as though he is sitting on your face and you can't breathe' (quoted in Alison Flood, unpaginated). In *Animal* Roth makes a decision to link the issue of male identity with the general issue of gender politics: while the older Kepesh is as manipulative as many of Roth's earlier heroes, his decision to allow Consuela to take control of her identity at the end of the book marks an interesting shift in power. As Debra Shostak suggests, she 'escapes Kepesh's point of view,' in using his skills as a photographer and his preoccupation with her breasts for her own ends, effectively reclaiming her identity even as she faces death from cancer. Shostak correctly sees this evasion of Kepesh's masculine perspective as disrupting and undermining his construction of self 'in terms of power and pleasure,' and ultimately challenging his history of 'detachment' ('Roth and Gender', 124). Some would say that shift in power comes early in the novel, when Consuela asserts her presence by biting at the hero's penis, or when he finds himself on his knees drinking her menstrual blood. Either way it is clear that in this book Kepesh must reassess his position in the light of a new threat both to his autonomy and to the psychological integration he has always craved: the inevitability of decay and demise. Thus the novel explores a theme that will be examined from a number of perspectives in Roth's late novellas. Mortality is an issue throughout the Kepesh trilogy, of course, particularly in *The Dying Animal*, and in Roth's late writing it is explored extensively. *Everyman*, for instance, presents an unnamed hero whose self-imposed isolation has similarities with Kepesh; like him, Everyman is both driven and partly destroyed by desire, and at the end of his life he must reflect on the worth of an existence founded on this paradox. *Exit Ghost* and *The Humbling* meanwhile construct aging heroes who also need to reconcile the consequences of age with the demands of desire. In the former, Zuckerman forgoes the opportunity of sex with a younger woman, seeking instead the consolation of art, but in the latter sex again offers apparent rejuvenation for the aging hero, Simon Axler. Like Kepesh, Axler is a performer—literally an actor—and the novel shows him to be locked in the familiar Rothian role of reductive masculinity; however, as with *The Dying Animal*, the book can be seen to qualify assumptions about masculinity, ultimately constructing Axler as the butt of a joke that underscores his abjection.

In one early interview Roth identified himself as a 'redface' writer, yoking together the terms 'redskin' and 'paleface' that Philip Rahv once used to describe divergent strains in American writing. The former utilise a colloquial voice, and look to low culture for inspiration; the latter are more cerebral, and have an orientation toward high culture sophistication. Roth saw his early career as a 'zigzag' between styles of writing that could be associated with these two extremes (see *Reading Myself*, 82-83). Thus earthy, overt comedies like *Portnoy's Complaint* and *The Great American Novel* (1973) might be considered redskin in form and feel, while the more stylistically restrained novels like *When She was Good* and *Letting Go* would fall into the category of paleface. Roth explained this clash of sensibilities in terms of his own background: as a child he was exposed to the 'redskin' vernacular culture of the Jewish working class, but in later life embraced the 'paleface' high culture of his liberal education. It will be argued that Roth's divergent voices first begin to find unified expression in the Kepesh novels, and in this respect these books set the tone for much of his later career. This shift in style is clearly evident in *The Breast*, and certainly by the time he completed the trilogy Roth was less associated with overt comedy, and more with the kind of restrained humour seen in the Kepesh novels. Arguably this becomes the dominant humour in Roth's work, and its legacy can be seen even in his twenty first century novels, where comedy relies less on Rabelaisian excess, and more on the kind of sophisticated irony and deep comic structure that first emerged in the Kepesh series.

So it can be seen that our study extends way beyond the Kepesh trilogy, offering a reading of the entire Roth canon that throughout will make connections to these three intense, exceptional books; it will show how, in our opinion, they constitute the pulsing heart of everything this extraordinary author has written.

Acknowledgment

The authors would like to thank Christopher Gair and Aliki Varvogli for their excellent advice during the preparation of this book.

The Rothian Dilemma: Early Stories

'Real Jews:' Goodbye Columbus

By the time Roth published *The Breast* in 1972 the theme of duty versus desire was well established in his writing. It can be seen in some of the early stories like 'Epstein' and 'Conversion of the Jews,' both of which were included in his first collection, *Goodbye Columbus* (1959). In the former the eponymous hero is dissatisfied with his conventional life and decides to take a lover; as is typical in Roth's early fiction, this rebellious gesture has unfortunate consequences. Epstein develops a mysterious rash, followed by a heart attack. The story ends with him in an ambulance as his wife pleads with him to 'live a normal life.' ('Epstein' in *Goodbye Columbus*, 229). Later in *The Breast*, of course, we will again see how a hero's transgressive behaviour can manifest itself physically. The child hero of the story 'Conversion of the Jews,' meanwhile, has a similar dissenting spirit. He argues with his rabbi over the possible existence of Jesus Christ, climbs onto a roof and refuses to come down until the adults have admitted that they believe in Jesus. His rebellion only takes him so far, however, and the end of the story sees him jump from the roof into a safety net, ultimately reconciled to the community.

Both stories depict heroes who strive to live life on their own terms but with limited success. Here and elsewhere in his early work characters who challenge community values tend to be thwarted, and their challenge is seldom seen in a positive way. His heroes are ambivalent dissenters, framed in stories that appear intolerant of individual demands and desires. Perhaps the clearest representation of this can be seen in the novella-length title piece, 'Goodbye Columbus.' Here Neil Klugman, a librarian from a poor part of town, starts a relationship with a member of a rich Jewish family from a salubrious area of Short Hills, Brenda Patimkin. He is drawn to her mainly because she offers a potential route to social advancement for him. However, she and her family are seen to be detached from their Jewish roots; they are disparaged by Klugman's own family as not being real Jews, for instance, having sold out to middle-class American society: as one character says, 'Since when do Jewish people live in Short Hills? They couldn't be real Jews believe me' (*Goodbye Columbus*, 58). Throughout the story Neil himself is critical of their excesses and their superficiality, and his desire to access their world is ambivalent; like F. Scott Fitzgerald's Nick Carraway in *The Great Gatsby* (1925), he is a parvenu, simultaneously attracted to and repelled by the world of the economic elite. As with Fitzgerald's hero, Neil is never truly comfortable in the world of abundance; when he is with the Patimkins he feels as if 'four inches has been clipped from my shoulders,' and has a sense of losing his identity, so much so that he needs to 'sit down in my Brooks Brother's shirt and pronounce my own name out loud' (66). The novel is heavily satirical and much of the humour is directed against the Patimkins, but not exclusively: we see the shortcomings of Neil's Newark background too, and particularly the paucity of his career as a librarian. Thus he feels ill at ease in both environments: he is unhappy with his social niche, but unable to leave it, at least not with a clear conscience. Though he fears the library will ensnare him, then, he never really feels there is a genuine possibility of escape; he anticipates growing old in this humdrum world:

> I … waited patiently for that day when I would go into the men's room … and … studying myself (in) the mirror, would see that … under my skin … there was a thin cushion of air separating the blood from the flesh … and so life from now on would be … a bouncing off, a numbness. (33)

Neil hates the library but cannot imagine a life outside it, and appears reconciled to developing the 'numbness' that might ameliorate the pain of it. There is a sense of inevitability about the ending of the story which sees Brenda leave her diaphragm in a place where her mother finds it. When the latter forbids her daughter to see Neil again, he accuses Brenda of having left it out deliberately in order to terminate the relationship. But given his attitude to Brenda and her world, there is some relief on Neil's part: her 'accident' effectively resolves his moral dilemma about whether to abandon his roots for Short Hills. At the end of the novella Neil is returned to the library, but while his dilemma may be solved, his dissatisfaction persists.

In one sense these early heroes want to make life conform to their expectations: they are dissatisfied with their lot, but in each case their desires are thwarted or curtailed, and the stories have a deterministic feel: the principal question is not if the heroes' rebellion will fail, but how and when. Invariably in these stories, desire creates moral conflict and the threat of alienation, and these themes preoccupy Roth throughout his career; they find their clearest expression in the Kepesh trilogy where, as will be seen, his departure from realism marks a crucial shift in how they signify.

'Real Men:' Letting Go

Roth's debut novel, *Letting Go* (1962), is also a story of moral conflict. The main point-of-view character is Gabe Wallach, the first of Roth's important lecturer heroes before Kepesh. Like Klugman and, as will be seen, like Kepesh, he is an ambivalent dissenter. It is suggested that he has inherited his duelling impulses from his parents' 'polar personalities:' while his mother is a woman of 'moderate emotions,' his father 'preferred the strange forces to grip him;' Gabe meanwhile describes himself as being 'pulled and tugged between these two' (45). On the one hand Gabe yearns to live a moral life: he admires his friend Paul Herz's moral seriousness, for instance, seeing his willingness to honour his obligations to his wife and family as indicative of his status as a real man. He wants to be seen as a 'serious' person, and he views marriage to a woman called Martha as a potential way of achieving this. The 'strange forces' he inherits from his father seem at odds with this ambition, however, and he never achieves the stable life he ostensibly requires. Martha's evaluation of men in general is a good assessment of Gabe Wallach: she says, 'Men want to be heroes. They want to be noble and responsible' (68), but they struggle to achieve this; certainly she recognises that Gabe's marriage proposal lacks conviction. It is merely a pose born of a performance of masculinity, rather than love. Like Klugman, Wallach is disengaged from society, and he lacks the requisite traits for genuine social integration. Martha sees that ultimately Gabe lacks the strength of character to make a good husband; his sense of duty will not translate into genuine commitment. Gabe is self-aware enough to see this too and, like Kepesh and numerous Roth heroes to come, he is plagued by guilt as a consequence: 'When I am about to die the last sound I will hear is my conscience cracking the whip' (220). Gabe is typical of Roth's heroes in that he knows how he *should* behave but always falls short of social expectations.

One of the most influential sociological studies of mid-twentieth century America is David Riesman, Nathan Glazer and Reuel Denney's *The Lonely Crowd* (1950) and it is interesting to consider Roth's early fiction in relation to this. Riesman argued that American society in the early twentieth century is increasingly dominated by 'other-directed' individuals for whom 'contemporaries are the source of direction' and who display 'an exceptional sensitivity to the actions and wishes of others' (21–2). In *Letting Go* Gabe is exactly like this, looking to his peers for models of behaviour and feeling duty-bound to please them rather than being true to his own instincts. Gabe's desire to emulate the seriousness and moral rectitude he associates with Paul Herz is a clear example. At one stage he tries to demonstrate to Paul that he is serious-minded, inviting him and his wife Libby to a dinner party with himself and Martha. The evening is a disaster because Martha doesn't dress as demurely as Gabe expects; he wanted to 'impress upon Libby and upon Paul—the seriousness of' his relationship with Martha, but she undermines this by dressing for dinner looking like 'some tootsie with whom I had decided to pass my frivolous days' (309). Gabe sees his relationship with Martha as an assertion of his maturity and masculinity; specifically, it represents what he feels is society's expectation of a man: commitment and seriousness. His 'other-directed' nature means that he needs his relationship to be endorsed by his peers; he needs 'just one couple to give us society's approval' (308). It shows of course that his relationship with Martha is about appearance rather than love, designed to give him social status. Ultimately both Martha and Gabe come to recognise this and the relationship breaks down; indeed, the novel concludes with Gabe in self-imposed exile in Europe: he cannot find it in himself to commit and suffers a 'dissolution of character' as a consequence (630). Where Neil Klugman couldn't satisfy his desire and returns to a life in the library, then, Gabe cannot satisfy his either and is forced to remove himself from his social world. Both are torn between conformity and dissent in environments that cannot seem to accept the latter. Later it will be seen that Kepesh, while more self-aware, and indeed more willing to step outside society's constraints, is no better able to achieve the psychological cohesion that all of Roth's heroes crave.

Frailty as Immorality: When She Was Good

Roth's next novel, *When She Was Good* (1967) examines the notion of duty and desire in a slightly different way. The heroine, Lucy Nelson, demands the kind of commitment and seriousness that Gabe associates with authentic masculinity in *Letting Go*. She marries what she feels is an ineffectual man, Roy Bassart, who finds it hard to meet her expectations. Confronted by his weakness—together with the general hypocrisy of life in her home town of Liberty Center—she begins to develop an extreme moral zeal. Jonathan Baumback called the novel a 'horror story about the Puritan ethic,' and Lucy becomes the embodiment of that ethic ('What Roth Hath Got,' 47). Like Gabe she begins to see simple human frailty as immorality and—though she perceives this frailty in others rather than in herself—the result is the same: she finds it impossible to function socially. Throughout the novel she berates people for their shortcomings, condemning them for hypocrisy and weakness. She becomes obsessed with the idea of the truth, forever measuring people against what they say, and often taking frivolous, ironic or empty words as statements of literal intent: as one reviewer said, Lucy is 'mad enough to take the old terms literally' (Geoffrey Woolf, unpaginated); unable to perceive irony or allow for flexibility, she takes everything at face value. Thus she cannot even tolerate the exaggerated stories her husband tells their child: 'what made her anger rise was not so much that the child naturally took them for the truth, but that Roy seemed to want him to' (*When She Was Good*, 215). Lucy develops a sense of moral superiority and self-righteousness, and constructs a perverse idea of what constitutes duty and obligation in a world where, as she sees it, duty and obligation are constantly shirked. As Maureen Howard wrote, 'Where there is simple human frailty, [Lucy] will invent sin and mete out punishment' (145). As a result, she becomes increasingly ostracised from the community, so much so that—again like Gabe—she is perceived as insane. Increasingly people cannot make sense of her—her husband says, 'what do you mean?' (*When She Was Good*, 281) and 'I can't understand you' (282), while Ellie screams at her, 'Nothing you say is clear' (280), and eventually, 'You are crazy; you *are*! You are insane' (303). Lucy's exile is more radical and permanent than Gabe's, however, as the book ends with her death. Society triumphs over the individual again in this novel, then, and throughout there is a sense of inevitability about this. Many critics have picked up on the Flaubertian feel of the novel, Jonathan Raban going so far as to call it 'a rewrite of *Madame Bovary*,' ('Bad Language,' 76), and as with Flaubert's heroine, there doesn't appear to be any way out for Lucy; it might even be said that Roth grafts his story so closely onto the pre-existing frame of *Madame Bovary*, that Bovary's tragedy, template like, determines Lucy's. It seems that an aesthetic orthodoxy—Roth's inherited storytelling model— reflects a moral orthodoxy at this point in his career. Certainly there is a clear tendency to privilege social, consensus values over those of the individual here, and there is very little sympathy for Lucy in the novel; indeed, the text seems quite hostile to her at times, leading countless reviewers to comment on Roth's negative treatment of her: the title of Richard Gilman's review of the book, 'Let's Lynch Lucy,' seemed a telling and accurate one for many readers (Gilman, unpaginated).

As can be seen, then, these early stories are informed by a notion of ethical duty against which the protagonists measure themselves and others: Neil is squeamish about embracing Short Hills life because he associates it with inauthentic Jewishness; Gabe cannot be comfortable with his inability to commit because of his constant ethical striving;

and Lucy cannot be reconciled to life in Liberty Center because she deems it corrupt. A sense of duty undermines Roth's characters' ability to achieve social integration, and this lies at the heart of what can already be seen as the typical Rothian dilemma. All of these characters become dissenters in their respective environments: Neil's longing for Short Hills puts him into conflict with the 'real' Jews of Newark, Gabe's inability to commit undermines his status among his peers, and Lucy Nelson's moral zeal clashes with the flexible morality of Liberty Center. Individual desires are at odds with social demands. As suggested, this conflict is central to the Kepesh books, and will be constantly revisited throughout his career; however, before we go on to discuss that in more detail, it is important to say more about Roth's aesthetic in this early writing, and particularly about the role realism plays in how the Rothian dilemma signifies.

The Limits of Realism

Each of these early books could best be described as realist in form and tone: *Letting Go* is often compared to the work of the early Henry James,[1] while, as suggested, *When She Was Good* has been likened to *Madame Bovary*. Certainly in each case the dissenting hero is dealt with in ways typical of traditional realism: invariably their individuality is seen as a threat to the status quo and is always ultimately thwarted. Just like the adulterous Epstein who is 'punished' with a heart attack, so Neil Klugman is disgraced for his sexual transgression when Brenda's mother finds her diaphragm. The failure of Neil and Brenda's relationship reaffirms the established social order. As suggested the question is not *whether* his relationship with Brenda will fail, but *how*. Both Gabe Wallach and Lucy Nelson suffer breakdowns and are at various stages deemed insane by the community; both are ultimately estranged from society: Gabe ends up in exile in Europe, and Lucy, like the typical transgressive heroine of traditional realism, is killed. Again both books have a deterministic

---

1   Some commentators have criticised it for this reason, suggesting that the style seems to stifle the story. Sam Girgus, for instance, says, 'By emulating Henry James [Roth] wrote a novel that most critics and reviewers deem desperately dormant.' See 'Between *Goodbye Columbus* and Portnoy' 144.

feel and happiness never seems a possibility. Importantly, where readers are meant to sympathise with, say, Kate Chopin's Edna Pontellier, Edith Wharton's Lilly Bart, Henry James's Isabel Archer, and countless other protagonists of early American realism, this is not the case here. Neil Klugman does not become virtuous until he has returned to the library, Gabe Wallach's immaturity is contrasted unfavourably with Paul Herz's ability to meet his obligations, while in many ways Lucy Nelson is depicted as a maladjusted shrew who gets what she deserves. Certainly in each case the desire that motivates them seems unsustainable in their fictional environment, and according to some this is an inevitable feature of the realist aesthetic. As Leo Bersani has written:

> Desire is a threat to the form of realist fiction…. Realist fiction admits heroes of desire in order to submit them to ceremonies of expulsion. This literary form depends for its very existence, on the annihilation or, at the very least, the immobilizing containment of anarchic impulses. (*A Future of Astyanax*, 67)

The idea of the 'annihilation' of 'anarchic impulses' is in keeping with the notion of closure associated with realism: at the end of a work of traditional realism the status quo is re-established and any dissent has been dealt with. This is the case in all of Roth's early stories. The hero of realist fiction is, as Bersani says

> defeated by a world whose victory we are invited to find both dispiriting and inescapable. The (desiring) hero of realist fiction supports a novelistic structure which includes his expulsion from the viable structures of fiction and life. (69)

Realism cannot tolerate/accommodate desire, and this can be seen clearly in Roth's early work. Indeed, this is an issue that Roth was acutely conscious of as he produced these early fictions. In his widely anthologised essay of the early 1960s, 'Writing American Fiction,' for instance, Roth discusses the problems American authors have rendering the experience of living in their country. He states that:

> the American writer in the middle of the 20th century has his hands full in trying to understand, and then describe, and then make credible much of the American reality. It stupefies, it sick-

ens, it infuriates, and finally it is even a kind of embarrassment to one's own meagre imagination. The actuality is continually out-doing our talents, and the culture tosses up figures almost daily that are the envy of any novelist. (*Reading Myself and Others*, 176)

Roth argues that writers were finding it difficult to do justice to the occasionally bizarre nature of modern American life as its extremes and complexities—its 'reality'—appear beyond capture. In a letter to *Commentary* discussing his intentions in that essay, he states explicitly that the problem for writers has to do partly with the perceived limits of literary realism:

> I intended to examine the relationship between our experience and our art, and perhaps come up with some reasons to explain the discomfort so many contemporary writers feel—myself included—with realism. ('Letters from Readers,' 248–52)

It is clear that Roth is reflecting on his own frustration with the narrative strategies at his disposal in the late 1950s and early 60s: he is obviously seeking an alternative mode of expression. As the 60s moved on, however, Roth does indeed begin to experiment with a different aesthetic. The stories that appeared in *Esquire*, *The New American Review* and *The Partisan Review* in the late 1960s had a very different feel to them, and ultimately formed part of the book that was to make Roth internationally famous, *Portnoy's Complaint* (1969). The Rothian dilemma features again here but it is treated rather differently. This novel is overtly comic rather than realist in form and tone, and as will be seen, the hero's dissent signifies in a completely different way.

Up Society's Ass: Comedy and the Rothian Dilemma

In *Portnoy's Complaint* there is a sense in which Neil Klugman's quandary is expressed in psychoanalytical terms. We mentioned how in 'Goodbye Columbus' Neil's desire for a materially better life clashes with his conscience, and such a clash is expressed here too, this time in the form of a battle between the id and the super ego. The hero, Alex Portnoy, craves a life of sexual gratification, but this is at odds with his conscience. His childhood has been dominated by a castrating Jewish mother who demands submission to her will in return for love. In the Portnoy household what is good is Jewish and what is bad is *goyish*: Portnoy soon begins to sense the ludicrousness of this but his desire to please his mother is strong and any rebellion is accompanied by profound guilt. Portnoy longs to free himself from his mother's will, and manages a degree of freedom via masturbation, which becomes an assertion of his independence and incipient masculinity. The freedom he craves most of all is freedom from guilt, but this eludes him because his Jewish upbringing has engendered such an acute sense of shame: he finds that 'every place I turn [there's] something else to be ashamed of' (*Portnoy's Complaint*, 50), and he feels like 'the Raskolnikov of jerking off' (20). He continues to rebel as an adult by having sex with *shiksas*, but again he cannot reconcile concupiscence with conscience and when his debauchery reaches its pinnacle with a *ménage-a-trois* between him, his *shiksa* girlfriend, and a prostitute, his guilt becomes physically manifest and he regurgitates his dinner. Portnoy's dilemma is portrayed as an inability to reconcile id and super ego, then, and this conflict is akin to those featured in earlier fictions. Portnoy expresses his own problems succinctly when he wonders if, like his cousin Hershie, he should capitulate to his family's wishes: 'how can I,' he asks, 'and still remain true to myself?' (65). This is the clearest statement so far of the Rothian dilemma: Portnoy's sense of duty conflicts with his instincts and, like other Roth heroes before him, this inhibits his viability as a social being.

It is worth considering Portnoy's predicament in relation to Lacan's distinction between the Imaginary and the Symbolic Order. The former relates to that pre-Oedipal period when a child feels at one with the mother, seeing no distinction between itself and the world; the latter is the post-Oedipal realm of symbols, language and the Law of the Father into which the child must enter to become a social being. Entry into the Symbolic Order severs the bond between mother and child and denies the child the object of its desire—the mother's body and Imaginary unity—which from hereon must be repressed in the unconscious, which is formed at this point. On entering the Symbolic Order, the individual acquires language and social position but at the price of submitting to the castrating Law of the Father, and the repression of desire. From now on the individual is a fractured being always desiring the lost wholeness of the Imaginary. Portnoy can be seen to have entered a Symbolic Order 'of orders' expressed, not by a castrating father, but by Sophie, his phallic, castrating mother. His neurosis is the result of his inability to reconcile himself to this world of division and deferred desire. Portnoy initially tries to define himself within the Symbolic Order—to conform to his mother's dictates—and does everything he can to please her. 'I roll the toothpaste tube from the bottom...say 'Thank you...'You're welcome," but he finds that this isn't enough. Her demands come to seem nonsensical and arbitrary and soon he begins to rebel: 'What law?' he asks, 'Whose law' (34); why should he 'conform to the norm;' 'Why should [he] bend' (103). Portnoy refuses to take up what he perceives is his allotted position in society. He refuses to marry and be like his father, a henpecked Willy Lomanesque figure: 'is there a law,' he asks, 'saying Alex Portnoy has to be somebody's husband and father?' (104). He cannot be like his father because he too is oppressed by the matriarch and this would also represent submission. Significantly, Portnoy finds some solace from Sophie's oppressive Law in the *shvitz* bathhouse with his father; this is a place where he does not have to think in terms of his mother's codes of behaviour; it is a place where he

loses touch instantaneously with that ass-licking little boy who

runs home after school with his A's in his hand, the little over-
earnest innocent endlessly in search of the key to that unfathomable mystery, his mother's approbation, and am back in some
sloppy watery time, before there were families such as we know
them. (49)

His enjoyment of the *shvitz* bathhouse demonstrates a desire to
regress to a time which predates the Symbolic Order and the laws
of the castrating mother; a place where there's no need to seek her
approbation. We are told that it is a place 'without *goyim* and women'
(49), and hence there is no need to define himself as Jewish (and thus
different), and there is no exposure to Sophie's law. This release is
transient, of course, and in everyday life his neurosis persists.

It is through language that the mature Portnoy seeks a cure—
the talking cure of psychoanalysis—but this proves extremely
problematic. Language is after all a medium of infinite metonymic
deferral, with its promises always beyond our grasp; and it is also,
as an expression of the Symbolic Order, a site of division. Portnoy
seems to embrace language via his linguistic exuberance, but
language is his oppressor as well as his intended route to liberation.
This is evident in his use of obscenity: Roth himself has said that
Portnoy is 'obscene because he wants to be saved' (*Reading Myself,*
19), and yet his obscenity augments his guilt; as Bernard Rogers
points out: 'by talking … dirty' all he really manages to do is
increase the guilt which binds and tortures him' (*Philip Roth,* 94).
Likewise, while the language of Freud defines his neurosis, this is
also the language of division (id/super ego), and it does not seem to
provide him with a solution to his problem. Portnoy's complaining
goes only one way, directed at Dr Spielvogel, whose single punch
line response does not offer a cure but, on the contrary, points back to
the beginning. Portnoy's incessant loquaciousness merely enacts the
metonymic movement of the ego along a chain of signifiers; as one
reviewer said, he 'simply moves sideways, like a crab, and in the end
nothing has really happened to him' (Hal Burton, 21). His is a wholly
lateral movement and his promised satisfaction is forever deferred,
continually beyond his reach as each word leads him to another, all
of them marked by absence.

The conception of the talking cure is different for Lacan than for Freudian analysts, as Fredric Jameson points out:

> For neo-Freudianism it would seem that the 'talking cure' is understood in terms of what we may call an aesthetic of expression and expressiveness: the patient unburdens himself or herself, his 'relief' comes from having verbalised.... For Lacan, on the contrary, this latter exercise of speech in the analytical situation draws its therapeutic force from being as it were a completion and fulfilment of the first, imperfectly realised, accession to language and to the Symbolic in early childhood. ('Imaginary and Symbolic in Lacan,' 358)

Thus, for Lacan, Portnoy's *Kvetching* would be seen as an attempt to situate himself within the social world, but this is impossible given the double-edged role language plays in his life: all it does is increase his sense of himself as a fractured being. There is nothing he can do other than opt out of language and society: Portnoy's howl at the end of the book is an attempt to relinquish the realm of language, to subvert the Symbolic Order. By the end of the novel Portnoy has given up on language and his howl suggests a desire for the pre-linguistic realm of the Imaginary and the unity that precedes division.

Up to this point, we have seen that Roth's heroes have a problem reconciling their instincts with the demands of society. In *Portnoy's Complaint* this effectively drives the hero out of society, with his cry of 'Up society's ass' (249), and his primal scream. What differs here is the extent to which the novel's humour seems to support the protagonist's decision to actively turn his back on society. The hero's dissent is not contained or curtailed the way it is in the earlier realist novels: Portnoy is defiant, and his defiance is underscored by his comedy in ways that privilege his dissenting views over those of his detractors—those representatives of society who would have him conform. Such detractors include The Monkey, who wants him to marry her, The Imaginary Judge who supports her in this, Naomi who thinks he should value his Jewish identity, his parents who want him to give up *shiksas* and settle down, and the Rabbi who insists he respects their views. Throughout he is seen arguing with these characters and in every case Portnoy effectively gets the upper hand.

The comic spirit of the book plays a key role in this. For one thing Portnoy is the only multi-layered character and without exception his detractors are caricatures, constructed by him as objects of ridicule. Freud said that caricature is 'directed against people who lay claim to authority and respect,' and that is the case here where all representatives of conformity are diminished and derided at every turn (*Jokes and their Relation to the Unconscious* 262). Take for instance Portnoy's exchanges with Naomi. Ostensibly she is the vehicle for some of the most potent criticisms of Portnoy's so-called selfishness and self-indulgence: he identifies her with his mother, and she becomes a mouthpiece for the community that expects Portnoy to behave but, despite the fact that she seemingly humiliates him by beating him up, she and her criticisms are effectively diminished in the text. Firstly, her name is an anagram of 'I moan,' and her speech throughout is presented as cliché-ridden ideological diatribe. She is also humourless—something liable to put one at a disadvantage in a comic environment. She accuses him of making 'silly jokes,' but the comic import of those jokes is augmented directly as a consequence of her humourlessness. At one point she is seen giving Portnoy a protracted lecture about his ideological shortcomings, and when she has finished Portnoy quips, 'Wonderful. Now let's Fuck' (*Portnoy*, 265). This may well reveal Portnoy's hostility and lack of sexual maturity, but in context it is an effective one-liner because its crudity contrasts so markedly with her status as a humourless ideologue; it becomes a pleasing corrective to her drab punctiliousness. Throughout the novel Portnoy delivers such put-downs with immaculate narrative timing and his comic monologue has a rhetorical import that his detractors cannot match. While at first sight Portnoy might appear to be a character designed to be laughed at, then, this is not really the case at all: he wins all of his arguments.

There is no discourse in the novel that is not mediated by Portnoy: effectively his voice *is* the novel and everything is drawn through his dominating consciousness. The story is presented as a confession, but the whole notion of a confession is shot through with contradiction. As Christopher Norris writes, '[c]onfessions are always ... a strategy designed to excuse the penitent by placing his guilt in a narrative context which explains it, and thus dissolves responsibility' (*Deconstruction*, 108). Moreover, while Portnoy is ostensibly a guilty dissenter, his guilt is only funny in that it is irrational, and in order for a sense of that irrationality to be maintained Portnoy must constantly justify his dissent. In other words, Portnoy is always right and his detractors are always wrong: in this way the individual and the individual's views are privileged. Many commentators have picked up on this aspect of the novel: Irvin Howe, for instance, felt that Roth's method 'Blot[s] out the possibility of multiple perspective'(73),[1] and L. S. Dembo writes of the 'monologism in which he is allowed to indulge by the psychiatrist's couch and as the putative narrator of the book in which he appears' (73), but perhaps Charles Samuels puts it most succinctly when he says that all Roth seems interested in doing in *Portnoy* is 'dropping stones on everyone but the hero' (1). Such comments attest to the fact that Portnoy's views are privileged in the novel—there is a clear sense in which we are meant to be persuaded by them at the expense of his detractors and society's representatives.

In the early realist novels, the protagonists' dissent and desire was meant to be seen as negative. In 'Goodbye Columbus' the reader sees the moral shortcomings of Short Hills affluence; in *Letting Go* the reader shares the community's sense of Gabe's weakness of character; and in *When She Was Good* the reader sees Lucy Nelson's moralising as absurd. Community values get the upper hand in these novels: it is the protagonists who are seen to err, and their estrangement, while dispiriting, is ultimately felt to be inevitable and right. In keeping with the spirit of realist fiction, their desire is contained. This is not the case with Portnoy, whose dissenting impulse is celebrated in the novel and sustained beyond its close.

The Breast should be read with these books in mind because, as suggested, it re-explores the theme of the Rothian dilemma in a fascinating way, and can only be fully appreciated in relation to these

---

1   Irving Howe's was an extremely hostile attack on Roth from an eminent Jewish critic who'd initially praised him. It was reprinted in his collection *The Critical Point* (1973), where he added that, after reading *The Great American Novel*, he had not altered his negative opinion of the author. Roth is thought to have responded to this attack in *The Anatomy Lesson* where he casts Howe as Milton Appel.

early novels. Roth actually wrote two other books before *The Breast* appeared: *Our Gang* (1971), and *The Great American Novel* (1973). Though the latter was published after *The Breast* it was, according to Roth, written before it.[1] This is significant in terms of Roth's aesthetic development. *Our Gang* and *The Great American Novel* are overt comedies: the former is a satire of the Nixon government, and the latter is a baseball fantasy which presents American history as a spurious narrative informed by corruption and conspiracy. It is not necessary to explore either of these books in detail here; it is sufficient to note they both have a similar feel to *Portnoy's Complaint* in that they are exuberant, Rabelaisian stories where Roth exploits his capacity for humour to the full. Discussing *The Great American Novel*, for instance, Roth describes his style as 'Satyric' in that it is born out of 'the sheer pleasure of exploring the anarchic and unsocialised' (*Reading Myself,* 36). This novel is told from the perspective of an old man called Smitty who claims to know the truth about American history—he has an alternative vision to the so-called 'Official Version of Reality,'[2] and sees the past as being underpinned by conspiracy. While Smitty's conspiracy theory may be absurd, his dissenting spirit is endorsed and celebrated in the book as offering a healthy corrective to consensus reality. As Ben Siegel says, 'Roth employs his hero's manic polemics to point up…what Thomas Edwards describes astutely as 'the plight of the truth-knower isolated by disbelief' (186). As in *Portnoy's Complaint*, the individual perspective is given a degree of privilege in this text. Where social demands dominate the early stories up to *Portnoy*, then, it's an antisocial, 'unsocialised' spirit that informs these 'anarchic' fictions of the very early seventies. As will be seen, this alters again in *The Breast*, and an aesthetic shift parallels a change in how the Rothian dilemma is expressed: in many ways this constitutes the most important development in Roth's writing.

---

1   See Bernard Rogers *Philip Roth*, pages 132 and 178. This chronology was purportedly pointed out to Rogers by Roth himself in conversation in December 1973.

2   This is a term that Roth used in interview to refer to the distorted representation of American life disseminated by mass media (see 'On *Our Gang*' in *Reading Myself*, 57).

The Turning Point

All is Oneself and Oneself is All: The Breast

Many critics would see the publication of *Portnoy's Complaint* as a key turning point in Roth's career as a writer: certainly it's here that he first finds a vehicle for his humour and his colloquial voice. His overtly comic aesthetic in Portnoy, and *Our Gang* and *The Great American Novel*, show him breaking free of traditional realism, and embracing a less constrained and more personal style. And of course *Portnoy* is the book that transformed Roth's fortunes as a writer, giving him financial security and an international profile. However, in our view it is the short novella that appeared in 1972 that constitutes the real turning point for Roth. As will be seen, it's here that Roth manages to achieve a degree of balance in his expression of the Rothian dilemma, and develops an aesthetic that becomes the perfect complement to his themes.

The Breast sees a Jewish professor of literature, David Kepesh, suffer 'a massive hormonal influx' which transforms him into 'a mammary gland disconnected from any human form,' and among other things the book charts his attempts to interpret his predicament (*The Breast*, 12).[1] It also details his fight to manage the intense longing for erotic stimulation which torments him, and in this respect Kepesh can be compared to Portnoy. Like Portnoy, Kepesh suffers from guilty sexual craving: on the one hand, for instance, Kepesh wants his lover Claire to perform 'the ultimate act of grotesquery' by allowing him to penetrate her with his nipple, on the other he is acutely ashamed of this desire and conscious that such demands might be excessive. Indeed, on one level *The Breast* can be read as a kind of surreal continuation—or even culmination—of *Portnoy's*

---

1   The book was later published in a revised edition, and when this edition is used it will be noted it the text.

Complaint, and several critics read it this way. It is worth considering how, for example, Ted Solotaroff's contention that '*The Breast* picks up where *Portnoy* left off' (178), or Melvin Friedman's view that it is a 'working out of certain fantasies suggested by *Portnoy*' (86–7) squares with the reading of *Portnoy* offered above. The desire among critics to establish such connections is indicative of how Roth will be read as his career develops: as will be seen, with many of his books, Roth seems to assume an ideal reader who is familiar with his *œuvre*; certainly his stories become richer when read in the broader context of his work, and his continuing preoccupation with the Rothian dilemma.

We saw how Portnoy is trapped by language: a fragmented being whose desire is infinite and infinitely, metonymically deferred. Lacan suggested that in the slide of metonymy lies the 'power to bypass obstacles of social censure' (quoted in Rosemary Jackson, 42), but in Portnoy's case this only takes him in a circle, back to the beginning (as Spielvogel says, 'Now vee may perhaps to begin. Yes?'). In *The Breast* the hero's metamorphosis can also be seen as metonymic. As Rosemary Jackson writes, in the process of metamorphosis 'one object does not stand for another, but literally becomes that other, slides into it metamorphosing from one shape to another' (42). In this sense Kepesh's metamorphosis looks like a symbolic expression of Portnoy's predicament. With this notion in mind, consider Jackson's comments on Kafka's story 'Metamorphosis': she argues that Gregor Samsa's transformation enacts 'a movement from self to other in a protest against oppressive reality, progressively withdrawing from society's humanizing schemes' (160). Portnoy too is oppressed by society's 'humanizing schemes' in the sense that they conflict with his instincts. In one way or another this has been the case for all of Roth's early protagonists. According to Lacan the Symbolic Order demands a spurious unity from the individual, a unity which can only ever be a performance because the desiring self is always at odds with the restraining self. For Jackson, however, the genre of fantasy—to which *The Breast* in some ways belongs—'makes an assault upon the sign of unified character' (87); that is, it creates a space in which the artificial unity of the Symbolic Order is challenged. Fantasy destabilises spurious social unity, asserting a different kind of unity: the authentic unity of non-difference. As Jackson puts it, fantasy

> expresses a desire for that beyond the Symbolic Order [which] unlike the symbolic … is inhabited by an infinite number of selves preceding socialisation, before the ego is produced within the social frame. (41)

The Breast expresses a desire to escape the Symbolic, reflecting a need for a non-social or pre-social realm. It is a craving for a state that allows undifferentiation or the free play of the subject's 'infinite number of selves' that social identity denies. Jackson writes that 'Fantasy has always articulated a longing for Imaginary unity, for unity in the realm of the Imaginary,' and in this respect Kepesh's metamorphosis serves a similar function to Portnoy's howl seen above. However, unlike Portnoy, Kepesh does not relinquish language; rather, like Gabe Wallach and Lucy Nelson who both suffer breakdowns, he finds it hard to make himself understood. He is in a similar position to Kafka's Gregor Samsa (whose voice is reduced to a squeak) in that it's increasingly difficult to engage with the world outside of himself: as he says at one stage, 'it is apparently difficult enough to make out my words when I am speaking loud and clear' (*The Breast*, 37). While Kepesh remains articulate, his voice is largely interior monologue and his ability to register in the world of social discourse diminishes as the story progresses. In other words, his transformation desocialises the hero verbally and physically, leaving him 'alone as anyone could wish to be' (19).

In a sense, then, the story becomes a kind of regression fantasy expressing a desire for a state preceding socialisation, and this is reinforced in several ways. Most obviously it is suggested in the simple fact that Kepesh becomes a breast, with all its connotations of pre-social unity with the mother. Also the abundance of water imagery in the novel underscores the notion of regression. At one point, for instance, Kepesh likens himself to an underwater mammal and feels he is being studied, 'as they would watch from a glass-bottomed boat the private life of the porpoise or the whale' (23); elsewhere he uses a diving metaphor to suggest a desire to return to infancy:

> I claw the slime at the sea bottom but by the time I rise to the
> surface there is not even silt beneath my fingernails. Ah, but the
> dive is invigorating…. I have returned to the earliest hours of my
> human existence … when the breast is me and I am the breast,
> when all is oneself and oneself is all, when the concave is the
> convex and the convex the concave. (63–4)

The ocean recalls pre-social, amorphous integration (undifferentiation), and the unity of the womb; indeed, in the diving image above
Kepesh explicitly identifies the unity he craves in terms that complement Lacanian theory. Though Kepesh's transformation marks a
symbolic expression of a desire for unity, however, this cannot ultimately be realised because, even though he has been removed from
society, he cannot abandon his social conditioning. As he says at one
point, 'not even *in extremis* have I been able to leave off determining
my worth in relation to others' (28). He sounds exactly like the 'other-
directed' Gabe Wallach here, of course, and he is also exactly like
Portnoy in that he remains governed by the conflict between libido
and conscience: his extreme desire for sexual gratification is coun-
tered by an equal desire to keep it in check. While at times he sounds
very much like Portnoy in full dissenting mode: 'Why shouldn't I be
… sucked and licked and fucked … if I want it?' (36), he also makes
explicit his need to achieve 'a victory over rampaging lust' (45). The
contradiction at the heart of the Rothian dilemma remains in *The
Breast*, then, and its hero's status as a breast is its perfect expression;
indeed, the conflict is embodied in the image itself given that the fig-
urative manifestation of his desire for unity takes the form of a dis-
membered body part. And this notion of contradiction is reinforced in
various other ways throughout the story. Kepesh often speaks in paradoxical terms, for instance, as when he suggests that 'there's madness
in being sensible' (37), and expresses dissatisfaction with satisfaction ('so much satisfaction frightened me' (66)); indeed, Roth himself has acknowledged that the book is 'shot through with contradiction' (*Reading Myself,* 73). In terms of gender too there is a contradiction: as Debra Shostak writes, 'Kepesh occupies neither male nor
female position,' and in part 'deconstructs the myth of male/female
bipolarity' ('Roth and Gender', 119). In this sense Kepesh as a breast

combines what are conventionally (albeit erroneously) seen as opposite: male and female. This contradiction, like all of Kepesh's contradictions, remains unresolved at the end. The Rilke poem with which the story closes constructs a final image of contradiction in the image of an Apollonian cripple. Here images of order and unity (Apollo's 'legendary head' and glowing torso) sit alongside references to disfigurement and death ('maimed and short').

The contradiction in *The Breast* is worth considering in relation to Julia Kristeva's notion of abjection. According to Kristeva we are simultaneously aroused and repelled by that which we cannot or do not wish to comprehend; we have an antithetical reaction to unpalatable 'excluded ground,' whilst at the same time it can be a route to the ecstasy of '*jouissance*' (17). In Kepesh's case there is pleasure to be derived from his peripheral status as a breast that, paradoxically, perpetuates his suffering. For Kepesh—the sexually driven male hero—there is perhaps a degree of wish-fulfilment in becoming the disembodied breast, the source of his erotic pleasure and fantasies since adolescence, which appears to enthral him and disgust him in equal measure. In this sense, liminality and abjection go hand-in-hand as his desire for the female mammary gland creates, to quote Kristeva, 'the scalpel that carries out his separations' (Kristeva 1982, 8), and perhaps created his metamorphosis—his liminal status—in the first place. Once 'adjusted' to his life as a breast, Kepesh makes light of it:

> My nipple is rosy pink in color. This last is thought to be unusual in that in my former incarnation I was an emphatic brunette. As I told the endocrinologist who made this observation, I myself find it less 'unusual' than certain other aspects of the transformation, but then I am not the endocrinologist around here. The wit was bitter, but then it was wit at last. (*The Breast*, 2nd edition, 13)

As soon as he is in a position to mock his liminality, Kepesh is able to derive abjected pleasure from it. In the following encounter with a nurse who periodically washes his 'face,' he demonstrates the adversative reaction of abjection explained by Kristeva:

> I could now feel each of her fingers touching me; then something was moving on me in slow, easy circles. The soft palm of her

hand. 'Oh, oh,' I cried, as that exquisite sense of imminence that precedes a perfect ejaculation pervaded my whole being. And then I began to sob uncontrollably and had eventually to be put to sleep. (*The Breast*, 2nd edition, 17)

Unable to ejaculate, he is forced to retreat into guilt and repulsion for enjoying the pleasures offered by his nipple. The binary gender oppositions that Shostak notes above are never more apparent than in this section: Kepesh is neither male nor female, neither human nor sub-human, but is both the subject and object of his own self-serving ecstasy. He wishes to ejaculate from a female nipple and comes so close to tasting that divine pleasure, but the realisation of its impossibility turns his delight into dismay, reinforcing his abjection and affirming his liminality. Following his daily washes Kepesh seems aware of his own abjection, explaining that:

> What alarmed me so about giving in to this grotesque yearning was that by so doing I might be severing myself irreparably from my own past and my own kind. I was afraid that if I were to become habituated to such practices, my appetites could only become progressively strange, until at last I reached a peak of disorientation from which I would fall—or leap—into the void. (*The Breast*, 2nd edition, 39)

The 'practice' to which he refers here is the desire to penetrate his nurse with his newly formed nipple. The 'void' meanwhile seems to be liminality itself; the traversing of sexual boundaries or 'thresholds' representing the point of no return which would require Kepesh to relinquish his status as a human being, thereby embracing his role as a 'preposterous organism' (*The Breast*, 2nd edition, 41). Kepesh's fear of indulging his abject sexual yearnings is related to his sense of identity. He maintains that, in succumbing to penetrating a woman with a nipple, he would 'go mad. I would cease to know anything. And even if I should not die as a result, what would I become but a lump of flesh and no more?' (*The Breast*, 2nd edition, 39). The thing which defines him as an individual is his ability to sexually perform as a man, not simply as a female form with a male consciousness; to entertain such extremes of abjection would be to invite psychological disintegration. Despite Kepesh's fear of abjection and disintegration, the need to find release through the nipple also implies a desire for integration. Ejaculation from the nipple can be seen to represent breastfeeding, which is suggestive of a time when mother and child are undifferentiated. For Lacan, desire emerges in the infant during weaning: when the baby loses the breast and begins to cry for food and affectionate contact, the absence of these things creates a space for craving. That Kepesh fails to ejaculate through his 'nipple' implies a failure to re-establish that former undifferentiated state, perhaps, and the continuation of the desire that torments him.

So *The Breast* presents Kepesh in a way that expresses his contradictions without the possibility of him resolving, transcending, or eluding them. The speaker's final words, 'you must change your life' make us wonder what choices there are for such a hero. The only option seems to be to oscillate between alternatives, the twin poles of his duelling psyche. The tension in the story is derived mainly from a single question: which will get the upper hand in Kepesh, self-indulgence or self-restraint? At the close of the novel that question remains unanswered, and this is where it differs from his previous stories.

As suggested, in Roth's realism there is a sense in which society gets the upper hand in the duty versus desire conflict: Klugman is returned to the library, and Gabe Wallach and Lucy Nelson are ostracised from society. These might all be seen as coming-of-age stories in the *Bildungsroman* tradition, but in each case the protagonist's maturation is stymied; the stories are all traditional realist texts which register society's inability to accommodate the dissenting/desiring hero, and each character's failure to satiate desire in the social context inhibits their development. *Portnoy*'s maturation is stymied too, of course, but here it's the hero who actively rejects his social world, using his comedy to justify his dissenting position and his final cry of 'Up Society's Ass.' Crucially, Kepesh occupies a middle ground between these two extremes. Roth's aesthetic in *The Breast* works to complement the dilemma, rather than privilege one aspect of that dilemma over another. Neither the individual's desire nor society's demands are seen to be endorsed here. Kepesh's story works to express and sustain his contradiction *as* a contradiction. As Jackson writes, 'the basic trope of fantasy is the oxymoron, a figure of speech which holds together contradictions and sustains them in an impossible unity without progressing towards synthesis' (*Fantasy*, 21), and Kepesh is himself an oxymoron, his incompatible drives manifest in his breast status and held perpetually is stasis.

The notion of a middle ground is also reinforced via the tone of the narrative voice in *The Breast*. Though Kepesh's predicament is potentially hilarious, his voice is by no means comic: there is none of Portnoy's incessant joking and Kepesh's monologue lacks Portnoy's spirit of self-justification which, as was seen, privileged individual dissent over the voices advocating social duty. As Frederick Crews suggests, Roth 'having chosen a storyline that looks ideally suited to his taste for outrageous sexual farce, has sidestepped the opportunity and instead written a work of high seriousness' (18); a similar point is made by R. Z. Shepherd who notes that Roth does not 'descend to the level of a vulgar joke. *The Breast* is more touchingly human than funny' (98). In *The Breast*, just as Kepesh strives to manage his desire and anti-social impulses, so the narrative is also managed and restrained. Though Kepesh concedes that there is a 'humorous side' to his transformation (*The Breast*, 35), he has to conclude that ultimately it is 'beyond comedy' (11); he certainly cannot justify or redeem himself through comedy as Portnoy does; he tells us that he longs for, 'A good belly laugh … a laugh starting way down at my watermelon end and swelling till it joyously trickles forth from the apertures in my nipple' (49), but it is not forthcoming. The restrained tone of the narrative as a whole is somewhat incongruous in the circumstances. This incongruity creates a mordant humour of its own, of course, but this is invariably qualified by sobriety: there is an uneasy tension between comedy and seriousness which again parallels the novel's central contradiction between desire and restraint. The extreme comic self-justification and defiant verve of Portnoy have been replaced by a voice marked by genuine self-reflection. Notice, for example, the many either/or constructions in the book ('Was I really so racked as all this by the indecent proposal I had made/Or was this hysterical episode for the benefit of my audience?' (37); 'Was I just another American boy raised on a diet too rich with centrefolds/Or was it rather a longing in me' (61), and so on). Where Portnoy's rhetoric was aimed at trying to convince the reader that he has nothing to feel guilty about, Kepesh's takes the form of a dialogue with the ambivalent self. This is one of the ways in which the novel emphasises the notion of unresolved conflict, and it sets the pattern for much of Roth's writing from this point on. The sense in which the either/or dichotomy is sustained is difficult to miss and vital to the development of Roth's aesthetic: the balance is paralleled by the tone of the book: its restrained humour rarely seems to have an obvious target, and while there is a joke at the heart of the story—a man as a breast—the complex irony means we are seldom invited to laugh either at or with the protagonist. Certainly this complexity undermines the views of those critics who deemed *The Breast* a one-joke book.

Importantly all of the stories preceding *The Breast* had a moral orientation or implicit point of wisdom in that they endorsed *either* social or individual values: in other words, in presenting the conflict between social and individual ideals the texts tended to sanction one or the other. Society's values have the upper hand in the stories preceding Portnoy: as seen, these stories re-established the status quo, and the desiring hero's forced conformity or expulsion is seen as appropriate, necessary and inevitable. The opposite is the case in Portnoy where the values of the individual are endorsed at society's expense; Portnoy's individualism is celebrated in the text and the representatives of society are seen to hold inferior views. In *The Breast,* by contrast, such issues are expressed in a non-hierarchical way. There is no discernible point of wisdom here, and where the former books could be considered imperative in the way they present the protagonist's moral dilemma, privileging either society or the self, *The Breast* has a more interrogative feel; it is much less sure of itself than the former stories. Hence it is significant that at this point in his career Roth should suggest that he is increasingly unsure of himself too: in an interview about *The Breast*, for instance, he says: 'For me one of the strongest motives for continuing to write fiction is an increasing distrust of "positions," my own included' (*Reading*

Myself, 71–2). Unlike the earlier novels, *The Breast* doesn't seem to have a 'position:' the book's import is far more reflective, analytical and undecided, seeming to parallel Roth's own inability to find a stable point of view. As Roth himself says, distinguishing Kepesh and Portnoy:

> Kepesh is lost—somewhat in the way Descartes claims to be lost at the beginning of Meditations: 'I am certain that I am, but what am I? What is there that can be esteemed true?' Unlike Portnoy, Kepesh is not interested in making his misery entertaining, nor is he able to bridge the gap between what he looks like and what he feels with wild humour. If Portnoy could do that, it was because he had less territory to cover. (*Reading Myself*, 71)

Here Roth seems to link Kepesh's uncertainty with a reluctance to employ overt humour; such an approach seems reductive because, unlike Portnoy, he has more complex 'territory to cover,' and this hints at Roth's own reasons for embracing a more restrained, subtle and interrogative voice: like Descartes he is not entirely sure what 'can be esteemed true.'

In some ways Kepesh displays characteristics akin to those associated with what David Stephenson called the 'activist hero.' In an article published almost ten years before *The Breast* appeared, Stephenson defined the activist as a hero with 'active self-consciousness [and] active self-awareness' who is 'an insatiable explorer of his own private experience' (338). Such heroes are embarked on a quest, a 'search for a sense of privately satisfying identity or self' and are concerned with their 'private irritations' and their own 'erotic needs.' The activist, according to Stephenson, is a 'caged self' and can 'never find permanent solutions to their problems' (240). Structurally too *The Breast* might be thought of as an 'activist' novel in that it is 'structurally indeterminate,' offering 'a feeling of conclusion only because it has exhausted our interest in the factual details of its characters' (239). It is the degree to which *The Breast* is 'indeterminate' that makes it such an important book in Roth's development. More will be said about the 'indeterminate' nature of the story later, and about Kepesh's activist status, but first it is worth explaining more about the role of Kafka in the novella.

'The Effort! The Work I Put In': The Breast and Kafka

Writing of the 'philistinism of interpretation,' Susan Sontag argued that there are 'three armies of interpreters' to whose 'ravishment' the work of Kafka has been subjected: 'Those who read Kafka as social allegory ... those who read Kafka as psychoanalytic allegory... [and] those who read Kafka as religious allegory' (656). *The Breast* has also been seen from each of these perspectives. Pierre Michel, for example, sees it as 'an allegory of man's plight today' (237); Elisabeth Sabiston suggests that it betrays 'mammary envy' and a 'desire to return to the womb' (32); and Jesse Bier maintains that it is in part 'a parody of the Old Testament' (220). This might suggest some parallels between Roth's novella and Kafka, then; certainly it is impossible to read *The Breast* without having Kafka in mind.

The idea of Kepesh's unresolved conflict is reinforced via the references to Kafka; indeed, there is a sense in which Kafka, and his themes of thwarted desire, stasis and alienation, are encoded in the text. Kafka is signalled clearly in the book's theme of metamorphosis, of course, and Kafka's tale of Gregor Samsa is implicitly invoked as an intertext. Kepesh as a professor of literature has taught Kafka, and through his own transformation claims to have 'out Kafka'd Kafka' (*The Breast*, 73). The idea that reading Kafka has caused his problem is suggestive of Portnoy: just as Freud created the language of division that produces rather than cures Portnoy's fragmentation, so Kepesh becomes a literal manifestation of Kafka's preoccupations; Kafka is culpable in Kepesh's story, just as Freud was in Portnoy's. We saw also how words reflect the division of the Symbolic Order for Portnoy, and the same is true of Kepesh; and, as some critics argue, for Kafka too. Kepesh feels that his reading is the cause of his problem: 'the books I have been reading inspired it,' he tells us, 'they put the idea in my head (55);' similarly, Martin Greenburg has written that Kafka's work speaks of a need to

> [h]eal the rupture between consciousness and existence [because when this occurs] the need for symbols—and for literature in general—apparently vanishes. That is one of the meanings of paradise for Kafka: the place where no books are. (50)

We feel that for Kepesh too, paradise would be a 'place where no books are.' In both Roth and Kafka there is a desire for the pre-linguistic, Imaginary realm. As Anthony Thorlby says of K., hero of *The Castle*, 'the liberty that K. desires is a pure spiritual freedom…an aspiration to emerge victorious over the monstrous process (trial?) of being a thinking, speaking person in a world where language doesn't even seem to apply' (63). We imagine that such a world would also be the ideal environment for Kepesh.

Arguably the themes most associated with Kafka are futility and intractability, and this is exactly what characterises Kepesh's life as a breast. Though he says 'I can't live like this any longer,' he knows that his analyst, Klinger, is right when he tells him he must do exactly that; and though Kepesh says 'I want to quit' his struggles as a breast, he knows that this will never be an option (22). He cannot abandon the struggle even though he senses that, like Josef K. in *The Trial* and K., in *The Castle*, the struggle will take him nowhere. The Rilke poem that ends the book states that 'You must change your life,' but change can constitute only vacillation between poles of behaviour. Kepesh the conformist and Kepesh the dissenter will forever be in conflict. This prospect of perpetual oscillation suggests Kafkan intractability: just as Kafka's characters' problems are never resolved, so we feel that Kepesh will remain on the horns of his dilemma forever. The story resembles Kafka in the sense that there does not seem to be an answer to Kepesh's problem: the hero's predicament is truly intractable.

The Breast represents a desire for unity whilst acknowledging the inevitability of fracture, and the latter is underscored via the form of the story itself, and specifically the openness of the narrative: what we are calling its interrogative feel. Again this suggests an affinity with Kafka: in his discussion of Kafka, for instance, Greenburg makes a distinction between narratives that possess what he terms 'unity of image' and those possessing 'unity of action.' While the latter are closed in form, offering a 'satisfactory,' reassuring ending, the former do not necessarily 'complete themselves in action,' but offer instead a unifying image: they achieve cohesion aesthetically by being centred around an idea or image (153). Discussing *The Trial*, he says:

[T]here is something inherently less satisfying about the modern unity of image.... Action narrative with a beginning a middle and an end *is* better narrative, because it expresses a completer life. Like the life of man which is its subject matter, literature needs to complete itself in action to be truly complete.... Spirit *and* action: they make unity of being. *The Trial* has aesthetic unity; but its aesthetic unity expresses the impossibility of unity of being. (153)

Like *The Trial*, *The Breast* fails to 'complete itself in action' and can be thought of as a 'unity of image' novel in Greenburg's terms: it has no closed plot, for instance, and terminates only because all of Kepesh's arguments seem to have run their course. It centres around an individual in stasis, offering little development and no sense of closure. The notion of formal disunity parallels the psychological fracture evident both in Roth and Kafka. Kafka's message, according to Anthony Thorlby, is that 'a man cannot consciously possess himself, i.e. be identical to his longed for fantasy image of himself' (*Kafka: A Study,* 78), and this conflict is sustained beyond the close of every Kafka story; likewise, for Kepesh, as Jones and Nance point out, 'no effort will reconcile the disparity between his mental self-image and the appearance he presents to the world' (94). Kafka's stories and Kepesh's story present images of fractured heroes that offer aesthetic unity (around the central image of the character), but this unity depends on the sense of fracture being sustained; it depends, in other words, on disunity of form, on the stories' resistance to closure.

It is interesting too that while all Roth's dissenting heroes struggle in their conflict with society, *The Breast* is the only book so far in which that struggle is *itself* seen as a positive thing. As suggested, Kepesh is an activist hero in David Stephenson's sense. This again is reminiscent of Kafka, as some people read him. For instance, Anthony Thorlby, writing of K. in *The Castle*, argues that 'By putting up a steady struggle against [the Castle's] confusions and contradictions he does achieve a kind of freedom' (*Kafka: A Study*, 70); elsewhere Greenburg argues that by changing the metaphor in his fiction from 'pursuit' to 'assault' the Kafkan hero attains a kind of 'moral freedom … a creative … transformation of his psychological defeat' (216). There is a similar salutary feel to Kepesh's struggle, both for meaning and for moral self-control in *The Breast*. Kepesh himself discerns this and it can be seen, for instance, when he strains to make some sense of his predicament: as he dredges 'the muck of [his] beginnings' in an effort 'to be sane and whole,' he is invariably frustrated, and yet there is satisfaction to be had in the struggle itself, 'Ah but the dive is invigorating! The effort! The work I put in' (*The Breast*, 63). Roth has said of Kepesh that he is 'the first heroic character I've ever been able to portray' (*Reading Myself*, 66), and the nature of Kepesh's heroism lies in his struggle. Like K.'s struggle to insinuate himself into the Castle, Kepesh's struggles appear futile, but the effort itself is ennobling and potentially liberating. The hero is heroic perhaps *because* his struggles are futile.

The whole notion of shame in *The Breast* is also reminiscent of Kafka; Greenburg, for instance, writes that Josef K. is 'ashamed before the judgement of the world. His freedom lies in shamelessness but he lacks the strength for that' (*The Terror of Art* (138)). Similarly, Kepesh, like most of Roth's heroes, has a deep sense of shame, and speaks explicitly of 'the shame of being seen' (*The Breast,* 19), as well as of the shame associated with his insatiable sexual desire (*The Breast,* 31). Freedom for Kepesh, as for Josef K. would be shameless-ness, but this will never be forthcoming, given the extent to which he is bound to social expectations.

So Kepesh's problem is a Kafkan problem, and Kepesh's claim to have 'out Kafka'd Kafka' is interesting in the extent to which it brings to mind Harold Bloom's classic study, *The Anxiety of Influence* (1986). Bloom shows how writers have a power relationship with their literary fathers, and clearly Roth can be seen in these terms. In *The Breast* he is writing on themes about which Kafka is the acknowledged master and his claim to have outdone his master can be seen as a rebellious attack of an 'ephebe' who, via a 'perverse wilful revisionism' seeks to undermine his literary forebear (30). In making Kafka literal—in other words in making Kepesh literally transform—and by self-consciously invoking Kafka, Roth creates a travesty of the Kafkan theme and asserts his superiority over the master: in Kepesh's words, 'Who is the greater artist, he who imagines the marvellous transformation, or he who marvellously transforms himself?' (82).

The idea of *The Breast* as being a travesty of Kafka is important, and while the similarities between this story and Kafka are plain, there are also crucial differences which require discussion. Firstly, with regard to the question of realism, the lucidity of Kafka's prose is often erroneously read as realism and it is worth noting that Kafka stories tend not to be realistic in the sense that Roth's is here. A relevant dispute between Adorno and Lukacs on the question of realism in Kafka is outlined succinctly by Alan Swingewood:

> Adorno argues that Kafka's narrative structures are only superficially similar to nineteenth century realist narration: the concept of time is problematic, the boundaries between the human world and the world of things become increasingly blurred. Kafka's style is not 'a specific form of a specific context' but the creation of a subjectivity which resists reconciliation with social reality. (129)

The corollary of Adorno's assertions is that Kafka's narrative technique 'undermines the reader's habit if identifying himself with the figures in the novel' (Alan Swingewood, *Sociological Poetics*, 130). Arguably this doesn't happen in Roth's text because the hero's world view *can* be reconciled with the real world in a manner that, say, Gregor Samsa's cannot. Throughout his narrative Kepesh invokes the reader's credulity and sympathy and is constantly striving to rationalise his position in ways that Kafka does not. Also the first person narrative strategy in *The Breast* invites identification where Kafka's third person, anonymous narrative does not. Another important difference between 'The Metamorphosis' and *The Breast* is that, in the former, the possibility that the hero's experience might be illusory is precluded: 'Gregor Samsa *awoke* one morning from uneasy dreams' [emphasis added] (89); in other words, he wakes from a dream into a world of, albeit distorted, reality. In Roth, on the other hand, the question of the reality of Kepesh's transformation is sustained throughout. According to Tzvetan Todorov this is one of the defining features of the fantastic as a genre:

> The fantastic requires the fulfilment of three conditions. First, the text must oblige the reader to consider the world of the charac-

ters as a world of living persons and to hesitate between a natural or supernatural explanation of the events described. Second, this hesitation may also be experienced by a character; thus the reader's role is so to speak entrusted to a character, and at the same time the hesitation is represented, it becomes one of the themes of the work—in the case of naive reading, the actual reader identifies himself with the character. Third, the reader must adopt a certain attitude with regard to the text: he will reject allegorical as well as 'poetic' interpretations. (33)

Kepesh's hesitation between reality and illusion is shared by the reader, while this is not so in Kafka's story. In *The Breast* readers can never be sure whether there is a rational explanation for events, and as Kepesh relates the horror of his predicament they share all of his misgivings about its authenticity.

Another important difference between *The Breast* and 'The Metamorphosis' has to do with the degree of self-consciousness and sophistication associated with Kepesh's voice. This, as will be seen, is one of several characteristics that might lead us to categorise this story as a work of postmodernism, and is another reason why it can be considered a breakthrough text for Roth.

The Mystery of Meaning: The Breast and Postmodernism

So *The Breast* is characterised by uncertainty in that the battle between conformity and dissent cannot be resolved; moreover, neither 'position' can be seen to be endorsed in this story as the text refuses to create a hierarchy out of the conflict between society and the individual. We saw above how this uncertainty is underscored by self-conscious, intertextual references to Kafka. Kepesh's transformation is not merely an attempt to create a metaphor for his predicament; rather it is related to the very issue of deriving 'meaning' from fiction. When speaking on the matter in an interview with Alan Lelchuk in 1972, for instance, Roth explains that this 'literary problem seems to me the human problem that triggers a good deal of Kepesh's ruminations. To try to unravel the mystery of 'meaning' here is really to participate to some degree in Kepesh's struggle—and to be defeated, as he is' (*Reading Myself*, 69). Such a statement clearly indicates that the reader is meant to identify with Kepesh's frustrated search for meaning, and see that search as a significant theme in the book. Ultimately we are prevented from deriving meaning from the protagonist's metamorphosis just as he is unable to explain or rationalise his predicament. As argued, a sense of this difficulty is reinforced with allusions to Kafka's frustrated heroes like K. and Josef K., and also, of course, Gregor Samsa. As we read *The Breast* we cannot help but recall the latter's stasis in 'The Metamorphosis,' which exists almost as an ironic Ur text for Kepesh's story: Kafka is playfully, comically reimagined in a way characteristic of postmodernism. In a sense, then, Kepesh is aware of himself both as an individual and as a 'text;' he is influenced by the works of the authors he admires and he uses their work as a touchstone for his own life. This suggests a postmodern reflexivity which signals Kepesh as both the fictional creation of Roth's and a collection of pre-existing intertexts, mocking the notion of originality and the search for meaning in a way that is typically postmodern. The philosophical uncertainty and the irony discernible in *The Breast* are reminiscent of literary postmodernism, then, and Roth doesn't just assert superiority over his literary master here, but also over his master's aesthetic: literary modernism. Roth presents us with Kafka's modernist theme of alienation ironically recontextualised in a postmodern context.

Fredric Jameson was one of the first theorists to try and periodise postmodernism, and he sees it as emerging

> [I]n the moment (the early Sixties one would think) in which the position of high modernism and its dominant aesthetics becomes established in the academy and are henceforth felt to be academic by a whole new generation of poets, painters and musicians. (178)

Kepesh as a professor teaching in the academy in the 1960s exhibits exactly this sense of modernism as 'academic' and redundant. He 'out Kafka'd Kafka' in that he underwent a literal metamorphosis, but so does Roth in the sense that modernism is no longer the cultural dominant. Andrew Ross suggests that postmodernism is 'no longer consonant with the dominant rationality of modernism and its...

commitment to find solutions in every sphere of social and cultural life'(x), and the same could be said of Roth's story. As seen above there is no point of wisdom in *The Breast*, as there is in modernist texts, and while there might be solace to be found in art for modernist writers, this is *not* the case here. Kafka's works exist as intertexts in the novel but in no sense do they provide answers to Kepesh's situation. Indeed, there are no authorities to be found and Kepesh can trust neither himself nor the world around him. Likewise, in the spirit of postmodernism, Kepesh is sceptical of modernist rationality, of either-or answers to questions of value, and he will no longer allow himself the luxury of truth. Consider also these words from John Mepham:

> Modernist fiction contains many voices, but they are orches-
> trated and controlled by one master voice which imposes its
> privileged interpretation on all the others. The text is, therefore,
> in spite of appearances, monological. The reader's will to inter-
> pretative synthesis is engaged and encouraged to give credence
> to this implicit monological discourse; the many interpretations
> are contextualised by it into one tonal and coherent meaning....
> Whereas modernist works ... display a heteroglossia within a
> unifying monological perspective [however] postmodernist fic-
> tion prefers polyphony as a positive principal; it is a pluralisation
> of worlds of discourse. (144–5)

The distinction Mepham makes between modern and postmodern could almost describe the difference in import between *The Breast* and the novels that precede it. Unlike Portnoy, who precludes any possibility of contradiction, Kepesh's monologue sustains its contra-diction; despite the fact that it comes in the form of a single voice, it is more akin to polyphony in its juxtaposition of irreconcilable positions. As suggested, where the earlier novels are imperative in the way they deal with the moral conflict of self-versus-society, *The Breast* is interrogative; there is a genuine dialogue between positions. We saw above how the narrative is full of either/or constructions and questions without answers. In short, Roth's writing in *The Breast*, and indeed in all his fiction from hereon, reflects 'the challenging of certainty' (Hutcheon, 48) that we associate with postmodernism.

There has been a postmodern shift is Roth's work, then, and this can be seen in the aesthetic complexion and philosophical import of *The Breast*. Dating the emergence of Roth's postmodern shift to the early seventies corresponds interestingly with Stephen Connor's dating of postmodernism as a concept that doesn't fully crystallize 'until about the mid-seventies' when 'claims for the existence of this diversely social and cultural phenomenon began to harden' (6). Before the publication of *The Breast* the concept had gained currency among intellectuals with debates about the problem of originality, the breakdown of consensus structures of belief, and so on, being had by high profile novelists like John Barth and William Gass. While Roth was not one of these early experimenters, he might be seen to be responding to a cultural shift that was already well underway by the time he published this novella, becoming one of the writers who contributes to this crystallization that Connor mentions. For Roth this continues with his next two novels, *My Life as a Man* (1974), and *The Professor of Desire* (1977).

Later in the decade Roth revised *The Breast*, and a new edition was published in *The Philip Roth Reader* (Jonathan Cape, 1981), appearing as a single volume in 1985. The changes were not radical, and most readers agreed with John Updike in seeing 'little improvement' ('Yahweh' 179); however, while Roth does nothing to alter the meaning of the book, the tone does change slightly and some of the alterations seemed designed to heighten the degree of literary self-consciousness. Where Kepesh relates his initial symptoms near the beginning of the story, for instance, the following is added in the revised edition: 'It was midnight, the time when transformations routinely take place in horror stories' (*The Breast*, 2nd edition, 5–6). Such changes work to augment the patina of irony in the story, and are in keeping with Roth's interest in postmodern literary strategies which, as will be seen, develop significantly throughout the seventies. In order to illustrate this, we will need to continue our chronological reading of Roth's *œuvre* and spend some time discussing his complex and fascinating novel *My Life as a Man*.

Useful Fictions: My Life as a Man

Where Kafka exists as an obvious intertext in *The Breast*, Roth's own work becomes an intertext in *My Life as a Man*, and the playful irony discernible in the former becomes even more a feature of the latter. He splits the novel into two sections, the first called 'Useful Fictions,' the second called 'My True Story.' The 'Useful Fictions' are comprised of two short stories starring the character Nathan Zuckerman. The first story, 'Salad Days,' is written in a light, comic style; the second, 'Courting Disaster' in a more sombre, restrained style. In other words, the aesthetic dichotomy associated with Roth's own early fiction is represented here: the 'Useful Fictions' juxtapose a comic story and a restrained realist story corresponding loosely to *Portnoy's Complaint* and *Letting Go* in their aesthetic affiliations. Bernard Rogers was one of the first critics to point out that Tarnopol's 'Useful Fictions' 'can be seen as a stylistic experiment on Tarnopol's part which mirrors a similar experiment in Roth's fiction' (*Philip Roth* 149–50).

The 'My True Story' section which follows the 'Useful Fictions' presents the autobiography of Tarnopol, the supposed author of these stories. This is offered as the facts which gave rise to the 'Useful Fictions'—i.e. the true story on which the fictions are based. Tarnopol's true story is essentially the story of his disastrous marriage to a gentile woman called Maureen, which is felt to be a virtually literal representation of Roth's own marriage in the late fifties to Margaret Williams, a claim Roth makes years later in his autobiography, *The Facts* (1989). So *My Life as a Man* is the story of a writer trying to make sense of his experience in both fictional and factual narrative. As Tarnopol is writing the so-called true story, however, he becomes more and more conscious of the fact that the truth slips away from him even as he tries to render it. It comes to feel like a fiction:

> Tarnopol, as he is called, is beginning to seem as imaginary as my Zuckermans anyway, or at least as detached from the memoirist—his revelations coming to seem like still another 'useful fiction,' and not because I am telling lies. I am trying to keep to the facts. Maybe all I'm saying is that words, being words, only approximate the real thing, and so no matter how close I come, I

only come close. (231)

Thus Tarnopol wonders where the truth can possibly be found: there is a truth of sorts in all of the narratives, and yet none seem to render the lived experience satisfactorily. Here again we have uncertainty, this time expressed in relation to storytelling itself: narratives are invariably limited and unstable. Tarnopol uses fiction and autobiography in order to try and understand his life, to evaluate his own behaviour in relation to what's occurred, but everything he writes never really captures the truth; if a 'real' experience can be communicated at all then it lies somewhere in the web of those narratives.

Roth complicates the relationship between fact and fiction still further by giving obviously fictional names to the characters in his so-called true story: two are called Lane and Frances Coutell, for instance, characters from Salinger's novel *Franny and Zooey*. He also constantly stresses that he cannot believe in his true story, calling it 'a farce' and a 'fairy tale' in which he is a 'performer' (304; 173). The spirit of postmodernism features heavily again here, then, not only in Roth's questioning the possibility of truth, but also in his metafictional approach to the novel. This is his most self-conscious fiction to date, indicative some would argue of a general trend in mid-seventies American fiction. As Tony Hilfer has written:

> By the 1970s the critical construction of postmodernism had shifted from black humour to fabulation and metafiction. Literature was being considered less in thematic, more in formal terms. In fiction, character, already diminished in black humour, is even more completely absorbed into the narrative voice and reflexively displayed as a vehicle of formal inventiveness. (127)

Roth's fiction has gone through a similar transition from the black humour of *Portnoy*, *Our Gang* and *The Great American Novel*, to the highly self-conscious metafiction of *My Life as a Man*. Here the hero of the 'Useful Fictions' is overtly signaled as a fictional construction; a product of Tarnopol's 'inventiveness.'

The self-consciousness in this novel extends to self-evaluation on Roth's part. In the 'My True Story' section Tarnopol gives his

'Useful Fictions' to various people for comments which are related to the reader, good and bad. The feedback reinforces the connection between Tarnopol's 'Useful Fictions' and Roth's own writing because it reflects the responses Roth's own fiction had from critics. One character loathes 'Courting Disaster' for its 'scrupulosity,' deeming it a 'morbid' product of a 'moral imagination;' he feels it shows that the 'conventional (rabbinical) side of (Tarnopol)...has a stranglehold on what is reckless and intriguing in his talent' (*My Life as a Man*, 117); this is criticism that could easily be levelled at *Letting Go*. Indeed, the link is strengthened by the fact that the story ends with the hero in exile in Europe, exactly like Gabe Wallach. At the same time 'Salad Days' is criticised by another character in terms that bring to mind much criticism of *Portnoy's Complaint*: she calls it 'smug and vicious and infuriating' and says 'I hate what he does with that suburban college girl...which is to twist her arm behind her back and say, 'You are not my equal, you can never be my equal—*understand*?'' (117–8). Thus his critics see Tarnopol as a 'Jekyll and Hyde' character, capable of aesthetic and moral extremes.

The two extreme aesthetic positions can be seen as value–laden in the novel: as with Roth's own fiction, one style is conventional and conservative (i.e. privileging society and stifling 'reckless' nonconformity); the other is dissenting (privileging the hero above those who 'can never be [his] equal'); one has a social orientation that privileges community values, the other is individualistic. Mikhail Bakhtin's thoughts on the way different types of expression (like different genres) can influence signification are worth citing here. Bakhtin writes:

> Certain features of language (lexical, semantic, syntactic) will knit together with the intentional aim, and the overall accentual system in one or another genre [and] certain features of the language take on the specific function of a given genre...knit[ting] together with specific points of view, specific approaches, forms of thinking. (*The Dialogic Imagination,* 228)

Bakhtin here is discussing how different styles of writing belong to different ideological registers and as a consequence have distinct ideological import. Something similar occurs in *My Life as a Man* where the styles employed in the 'Useful Fictions' connote, as it were, specific attitudes to life—certainly that is so in 'My True Story,' where readers associate realism with convention and rabbinicalness, and comedy with viciousness and recklessness. Also the styles carry additional freight for the informed reader of *My Life as a Man* because of the relationship with Roth's own career and how this has been perceived. They signal Roth the serious and conservative writer of restrained realism on the one hand, and Roth the shocking and rebellious writer of wild and 'pornographic' comedy on the other. So this novel constitutes self-reflection of an extreme kind. In 1987 Tony Tanner argued that 'a lot of contemporary American fiction … is turning modes of discourse into objects of discourse,' and thus giving them 'visibility' they would not formerly possess' (*Scenes of Nature, Signs of Life* 176–7). This, according to Tanner, allows readers to engage critically with contemporary discourses where normally they would be blind to their conventions. Similarly, Roth is able to point to and interrogate divergent ways of telling by turning them into objects of discourse for the reader. Thus there is a sense in which *My Life as a Man* becomes what Bakhtin might call dialogical in two ways: two distinct styles of writing are set in opposition within the novel, but also, because the 'Useful Fictions' can be seen as stylised expressions of the author's (Roth's) former aesthetic, they also have a dialogical relationship with Roth's own fiction, adding another layer of complexity to the novel. In the same way, the 'My True Story' section—the so-called autobiographical piece—adds still more irony to this relationship, existing as it does in self-conscious reflexive relation both to the 'Useful Fictions' *and* to Roth's own life and fiction. He uses the novel to ironically evaluate his own aesthetic and moral preoccupations. There is a balancing of what Roth terms the 'redskin' and the 'paleface' aspects of his authorial sensibility. To modern ears these terms have a slightly racist feel, and no doubt Roth would be inclined to avoid them; as suggested above, however, he borrows them from a 1930s essay by Philip Rahv, and, as they are useful in helping us understand Roth's literary sensibility, it is worth saying a little more about them here. In his assessment of American literary history, Rahv identified an opposition between earthy, colloquial voices on the one hand, and refined, sophisticated, more constrained and conservative voices on the other. The former, 'redskin' voice, he associated with quintessentially American writers like Walt Whitman and Mark Twain; the latter 'paleface' voice with writers such as Henry James and T. S. Eliot. Discussing this distinction in interview, Roth himself suggests that where the redskin can express 'the vitality… of the people,' on the one hand, he can also be 'anti-intellectual' on the other; likewise, where the paleface moves in 'an exquisite moral atmosphere,' on the one hand, he can also be 'snobbish' on the other (*Reading Myself*, 82). Roth identifies this divergence in himself and feels that it reflects a clash of cultures associated with his background and development as a writer. Roth's working-class upbringing in Newark of the 1930s facilitated the development of the redskin: in this predominantly Jewish neighbourhood he was exposed to the Jewish colloquial voice and developed a feel for its rhythms and its humour. However, like many growing up in mid-century America Roth had the chance to go to University, study English literature, and experience a different kind of life and culture. This enabled the development of the paleface in Roth. To reflect this 'reconciliation' of opposites, Roth describes himself as a 'redface' (*Reading Myself*, 83). However, the reconciliation gave rise to what he describes as a 'deliberate zigzag' in his writing between the two: moving from the constrained realism of the early work to the overt comedy of the late 1960s and early 1970s. In *The Breast* we saw a synthesis between the two voices and what they represent; importantly this is where the so-called redface Roth first emerged as an amalgam of opposite sensibilities and styles; this might be said to reflect a more balanced representation of the conflict between the hero's position and the obligations associated with tradition and responsibility. In the first section of *My Life as a Man*, 'Useful Fictions,' Roth juxtaposes this creative and emotional conflict, and in the 'My True Story' section he once more presents the kind of redface synthesis first seen in *The Breast*. Again this reflects the spirit of postmodernism—the merging constitutes a closing of the gap between cultures and styles, and an adoption of a non-hierarchical approach to the moral implications (duty versus desire) that these styles seem to have in Roth's fiction.

Roth's preoccupations in *The Breast* and particularly *My Life as a Man* suggest a culturally eclectic, postmodern attitude in that they embrace both high and low cultures: the high art and refinement of the paleface, and the folksy comedy of the redskin; more generally they also correspond to a spirit of cultural synthesis that some critics have identified with the 1970s. For instance, Daniel Snowman has written of the conflict of styles and sensibilities discernible in 1960s America (culture versus counter culture; conservative versus liberal) finding resolution in the 1970s:

> The new atmosphere of the 1970s represented a fusion, a new synthesis of the two adversary cultures of the 1960s…the integration of two hitherto opposing tendencies. (293)

So the fusion that Roth achieves in *The Breast* continues in *My Life as a Man* in a way that reflects broader aesthetic and cultural shifts in the States in the late 1970s.

Putting on Her Underpants: The Unifying Urge

We saw how the central symbol of *The Breast*—Kepesh as a mammary gland—expresses a desire for unity, yoking together the conflict at the heart of the hero's trauma and offering an eloquent symbolic expression of his dilemma. Something similar happens in *My Life as a Man*. Like Kepesh, Tarnopol also craves unity: as the author of such divergent fictions he is torn emotionally between the conformity of 'Courting Disaster' and the dissent of 'Salad Days;' likewise in life he is conflicted between duty and self-interest: in his relationship with Maureen he is like Gabe Wallach who knows what convention tells him he *should* do, but who cannot reconcile this with his desire. He is 'duty bound' to the woman in his life on the one hand, but emasculated by her demands on the other. Thus it is interesting that when Tarnopol feels this conflict most intensely he should don his wife's clothes: 'I put on a pair of her underpants…Then I tried to get into one of her brassieres' (*My Life as a Man*, 210). Here again Roth provides us with a symbolic representation of the hero's conflict, this time expressed in terms of gendered clothing: the dissenting male and the emasculating female are brought together in the single image of Tarnopol in women's underwear: the male desire for freedom and the female demand for conformity are juxtaposed; they are combined as an expression of the unity that Tarnopol craves. In life, however, Tarnopol can never be anything other than a fragmented being; his dilemma will never be resolved. Thus even when Maureen—his principal 'nemesis'—is killed, it is clear his trauma will continue: he tells us that he is 'released' but not 'free,' and twice asks himself 'has anything changed?' (101; 138). The answer is no; Maureen may be dead and gone but Tarnopol has a new woman in his life by this stage and she also desires marriage, implicitly demanding he commit to her: 'Oh, my God, I thought—now you. You being you! And me! This is me who is being me and none other!' (330). Tarnopol's problems will persist if he is to continue to be himself. Unlike Gabe Wallach, however, Tarnopol is self-aware enough to realise that any attempt at conformity would be a performance: thus in his relationship with Maureen he had 'no more sense of reasonable alternatives than a character in a melodrama or a dream' (125). Conformity and nonconformity are incompatible but mutually alluring positions for Tarnopol, and they can never be reconciled in anything other than a symbolic way (Tarnopol in drag); if he is to be true to himself he has to acknowledge both aspects of his character and accept that a struggle between the two is an inevitable part of life.

As with Kepesh, however, there is a degree of nobility in Tarnopol's struggle: like Kepesh, Tarnopol will continue to try to make sense of his life even though the truth will evade him. Though he cannot articulate truth either in fiction or autobiography, the compulsion itself offers a kind of truth: 'At any rate, all I can do with my story is tell it. And tell it. And tell it. And *that's* the truth' (231). This idea that storytelling offers the only meaningful way of understanding the world links *My Life as a Man* both to *The Breast* and *The Professor of Desire*. This is how Kepesh the scholar reads Kafka's stories in the former, for instance, and, as will be seen, it is how he relates to Chekhov in the latter: while Kepesh cannot see salvation in art, it is nevertheless one of the few valid expressions of the human predicament.

A Rake Among Scholars: *The Professor of Desire*

The Professor of Desire re-employs some of the characters of *The Breast*, re-examines its themes and reconstructs the familiar conformity/dissent paradigm. It serves as a prequel to *The Breast*, addressing Kepesh's pre-metamorphosed life. Charting the development of Kepesh's psychological ambivalence, it once more frames a story of disruptive and unquenchable desire. It is a more substantial and arguably more sophisticated treatment of this theme than *The Breast*, however, as several reviewers noted: Paul Gray in *Time* called it, 'a more thoughtful handling' of his early theme' (78); Vance Bourjaily praised it as 'stylistically elegant' (1); and Larry Simonburg noted that Roth has, 'refined away excess effect, eschewing the easy joke and burst of colourful language in favour of clarity and understatement; he has matured'(unpaginated). It does indeed have a refined and considered feel, and it develops Roth's interest in the kind of self-consciousness and intertextuality seen in *The Breast* and in *My Life as a Man*.

The psychodynamics of desire and restraint once more lie at the heart of this book, then, and find clear expression in the title: Kepesh is a 'professor of desire' whose desire for an ordered, scholarly life is constantly under threat of disruption from an irrepressible id and a penchant for danger. Many of the characters can be categorised according to whether they appeal to the conformist or the dissenter in Kepesh. For instance, Herbie Bratasky, whose crude humour and 'shameless exhibitionism' captivate Kepesh as a child (*Professor*, 4), is clearly associated with the latter. It is not so much Herbie's ability to 'simulate the panoply of sounds—ranging from the faintest springtime sough to…diarrhoea' (6–7), but his desire to perform them in public that appeal to the young Kepesh. Sitting in opposition to this are Kepesh's parents, particularly his 'Mosaic dad' who censors Bratasky accordingly, 'Oh spare me, Bratasky, please…Don't you realize these are people who keep kosher? Don't you get it about women and children? My friend, it's simple—the shofar is for the High Holidays and the other stuff is for the toilet. Period, Herbie. Finished' (6). Kepesh is drawn to Herbie's low comedy at a price, then, and he feels that if he maintains contact with him

> My mother and father would be shamed forever. The Hungarian Royale will lose its good name and go bankrupt. Probably I will not be allowed to be buried within the cemetery walls with the other Jews. (8)

This naïve fear of moral estrangement parallels in an exaggerated form the sense of social alienation that plagues Roth's dissenting heroes from Klugman through to Tarnopol. Herbie Bratasky is more than Kepesh's childhood hero: he represents his unruly id, and he re-emerges later in the novel—most notably in the dream sequence with Kafka's whore—like the return of the repressed. When Kepesh reaches college he indulges his desire for play still further by joining the drama society. Initially this appeals to his Portnoyesque 'egomaniacal craving for the spotlight and applause' (11), but the more Kepesh is exposed to serious study the more he feels the need to be disciplined. He comes to feel that acting is narcissistic and self-indulgent and, like comedy, frivolous. He undergoes a transformation at college as the professorial, conformist facets of his personality begin to take precedence; he tells us that 'the next me—turns out to be a sober, solitary rather refined young man, devoted to European literature' (12).

While study and sobriety equate to harmony and stability for Kepesh, the lure of sex and adventure are never far away, and these find expression in his adult life via characters like Baumgarten, the 'rake among scholars' who teaches alongside Kepesh at the University (17). Baumgarten is the antithesis of establishment scholars such as Schonbrunn, another of Kepesh's colleagues; while the latter is sober and sensible, the former is shameless in his love of sex. Baumgarten has thus 'earned the disdain' of his 'colleagues and their wives' in that he stands in opposition to their 'standards of propriety and respectability' (123). Such is his appeal to Kepesh that the latter dubs him his 'alter ego' (126), underscoring the point that transgression is integral to Kepesh's character. Kepesh's conflict is also manifest in his love life. This is apparent initially in the contrasting temperaments of Birgitta and Elisabeth, the women he meets whilst studying abroad in England; as Robert Alter writes, the former becomes 'the polymorphous accomplice to the dangerous id,' with Kepesh attracted to her 'unfathomable and wonderful daring;' the latter, by contrast, is 'linked with refuge and order, with eros assimilated to the demands of the superego' ('The Education of David Kepesh,' 479). Where Birgitta is the dissenting match, then, Elisabeth is the potential conformist mate and he is attracted to her 'unfathomable and wonderful love' (47). While the latter would provide a route to domesticity and be adored by his parents, the former is an exciting but chaotic force. Birgitta disrupts his studies, and when he finally makes up his mind to manage his desire and leave her in Europe, it is because he wants to 'resume [his] serious education' (49). Birgitta and Elisabeth anticipate and parallel the conflicting traits of Helen and Claire who, in terms of their appeal to Kepesh, are dissenting and conformist females respectively. Helen is Kepesh's first wife and he cannot achieve a stable life with her: she chides him for his 'professorial smugness and prissiness' (71) and her behaviour disrupts his attempts to live seriously. She is beautiful and he has a powerful desire for her, but ultimately he tells us that she 'dissolves' 'the hold I had on myself' (93). She is antithetical to the conformist Claire who, Kepesh tells Kilinger, '"is to steadiness" ... "what Helen was to impetuosity"' (158). So the novel shows Kepesh to be torn between two opposing female types; what he calls the 'furnace and the hearth' (47).

In his early life Kepesh partakes of the 'furnace' and suffers the consequences when he has a breakdown following his marriage with Helen; it is not until he meets Claire that he achieves a modicum of stability. At first with Claire he feels that he might achieve a unity of opposites: he sees her as a woman who could fulfil all his needs as a so-called professor of desire. In the early stages of their lovemaking, for instance, we are told that he 'was a little bit of a beast,' she 'a little bit of a tramp' (199). Always he aspires to reconcile the conformist and dissenting aspects of his character; thus he asks at one stage:

> Is there not a point on one's way when one yields to duty, wel-
> comes duty as once one yielded to pleasure, to passion, to adven-
> ture—a time when duty is the pleasure, rather than pleasure the
> duty. (253)

Kepesh seeks to unify what for him are opposites, duty and pleasure.
Though they do achieve a unity of sorts during the initial stages of his
time with Claire, readers of *The Breast* will know that there is never a
possibility of Kepesh enjoying the equilibrium he needs.

The impossibility of Kepesh achieving psychological integration
is signalled in several ways, most obviously in that this is a prequel
to a novella in which Kepesh becomes a breast: informed readers
will clearly relate everything to their knowledge of Kepesh's
trajectory beyond the close of the book. Though Roth played down
the significance of this in interview, suggesting that readers shouldn't
'draw any direct connections between the two books,'[1] the parallels
can hardly be overlooked. Indeed, the close of the novel clearly points
us in that direction:

> I raise [Claire's] nightgown ... and with my lips begin to press
> and tug her nipples until the pale, velvety, childlike areole erupt
> in tiny granules and her moan begins. But even while I suck in
> desperate frenzy at the choicest morsel of her flesh ... I pit all my
> accumulated happiness and all my hope against transformations
> yet to come. (*Professor*, 262–3)

The breast imagery, the language of metamorphosis, and the
implication of Kepesh's final actions are intensely significant to
informed readers: it is a clear allusion to his impending metamorphosis
which asserts the intractability of the hero's dilemma.

The sense that Kepesh's happiness will be transient is underscored
also via the apple imagery in the final scenes of the novel. The end of
summer is heralded by 'the first of the ripe apples dropping onto the
grass in the orchard just beyond the house' (250), and shortly after
Kepesh likens Claire's face to an apple: 'so apple-smooth, apple-
small, apple-shiny, apple-plain, apple-fresh' (251). Later Kepesh
evokes the image of a falling apple to describe his own unease. At

---

1   See for instance, Sara Davidson, 'Talk With Philip Roth,' 51.

the moment when he becomes most aware of his love for Claire and feels 'the true self at its truest, moored by every feeling to its own true home,' he is still blighted by doubt and feelings of dislocation. Thus, like a falling apple he

> [C]ontinues to imagine that he is being drawn away by a force as incontrovertible as gravity.... As though he is a falling body, helpless as any apple in the orchard which has broken free and is descending towards earth. (255)

Like the summer, Kepesh's happiness will be coming to an end soon: the inevitability of his fall away from the 'apple-fresh' Claire is clear enough. The grammatical shift to the third person in this passage undermines the hero's assertion that he is, as he thinks, 'implicated in his own life;' rather it heralds the time when he will be torn free of his mooring to his 'own true home'—Kepesh, who has throughout been at the first-person centre of his narrative, is grammatically dislocated here just as he is soon to be emotionally dislocated and the helpless victim of forces he can neither fathom nor control.

At the end of the story the sense of impending disorder is suggested also by the return of those characters who have been the most disruptive in Kepesh's life. He receives a request for a job reference from the renegade poet, Baumgarten, while his father brings news of his old childhood idol, Bratasky. Most unsettling of all for Kepesh is the appearance of his ex-wife Helen. She arrives with her new husband to remind Kepesh that he is her 'dear old comrade' (216); she tells him that she is already growing apart from her new husband and wonders if Kepesh, as her kindred spirit, is entirely content with Claire: 'Doesn't she drive you even the least bit crazy being so bright and pretty and good?' (217). It is significant of course that this question remains unanswered.

'Frustration of Illusions:' Kepesh and Chekhov

It is important that Kepesh is a Chekhov scholar, and the way Chekov's work signifies in the book is central to how we interpret it. Certainly the inevitability of Kepesh's continued unhappiness is underscored via the numerous Chekhovian references. Roger

Hingley, for instance, argues that 'anti-climax, and the frustration of illusions,' are 'basic to Chekhov's art,' and time and again characters in Chekhov's stories are shown as having made the wrong pivotal life decisions (see Chekhov, *Eleven Stories*, x). At least this is so in the stories Kepesh himself cites in *Professor*. In 'About Love,' for example, the hero is shown in a state of regret having given up his true love, while 'Gooseberries' is about a man who, driven by pointless and pernicious ambition finds that his life has been wasted worrying about nothing more significant than a plot of gooseberries. Their themes of frustration and blindness parallel both Kepesh's inability to fathom his own heart and his fear of making the wrong decision. Discussing these three particular stories Hingley says,

> all three stories denounce the tendency whereby, in Chekhov's view, human beings tend arbitrarily to fetter themselves with superfluous encumbrances—ideology, ambition, love—thus renouncing man's most precious birth right, freedom.' (Chekhov, x)

Thus the Chekhov allusions complement and potentially consolidate our sense of Kepesh's own desire to

> [S]eek a way out of the shell of restrictions and convention, out of the pervasive boredom and stifling despair, out of the … endemic social falsity, into what [Chekhov's heroes] take to be a vibrant and desirable life. (*Professor*, 156)

Moreover, the Chekhov references work to strengthen the feeling that Kepesh himself, like Chekhov's characters, will never fully overcome the lure of the 'vibrant and desirable life.' Kepesh fears that if he were to marry Claire, he would become like one of Chekhov's 'well-bred wives … who during dinner with the guests wonder, "why do I smile and lie?"' (156). The Chekhovian sense of imminent disenchantment is shown most forcefully at the close of *Professor* where Kepesh and Claire's life seems to take the form of a typical Chekhov tale. As he describes his father's visit to their seemingly idyllic retreat he refers to it as

> A simple Chekhov story called 'The Life I Formerly Had.' Two old men come to the country to visit a healthy, handsome young

couple brimming over with contentment…. They are in love. But after dinner by candlelight one of the old men tells of his life, about the utter ruination of the world, and about the blows that keep coming. And that's it. The story ends [with the couple] wondering what they have to fear…. 'And both of them knew that the most complicated and difficult part was just beginning'. (*Professor*, 260)

The final line—suggesting the threat of impending disillusionment—is the concluding line of Chekhov's 'Lady With a Lapdog.' Clearly Roth uses Chekhov to undermine the notion that Kepesh and Claire will achieve lasting happiness, and he does so in a way that ironically acknowledges the influence of Chekhov. In that it reworks a well-used literary theme, Roth's overt intertextuality here might be said to reclaim a literary cliché, and in this respect is indicative of postmodernism's relationship with the already written as described by Umberto Eco, amongst others. By acknowledging Chekhov, Roth is signalling his debt to pre-existing texts, and to the exhausted themes and plots that he as a writer is forced to reuse. He is signalling his literary sophistication and at the same time ensuring that, in Eco's words, 'irony, metalinguistic play [and] enunciation [are] squared,' in a manner that offers an 'ironic rethinking' of Chekhov (227).

Chekhov is a communicative symbol in this book which for an informed reader adds another dimension to Kepesh's dilemma, and particularly his struggle to be free of the trauma this creates. Kepesh struggles for change in his life and despite the inevitability of stasis there is dynamism in his engagement with his duelling impulses and quest for emotional stability. As Robert Alter rightly says, it is 'a novel about the painful attempt to grow up…to confront one's own nature, to make some kind of coherence in one's life' ('The Education of David Kepesh,' 480). This is a key theme of Chekhov too; indeed, the title of Alter's review, 'The Education of David Kepesh,' alludes to a 1955 article on Chekhov's writing by Philip Rahv called 'The Education of Anton Chekhov.' Rahv's article is interesting because it seems likely that it influenced Roth's treatment of Chekhov in *Professor*. For instance, Rahv makes specific reference to the story 'Man in a Shell' which Kepesh takes for the title of his book on

Chekhov. Rahv identifies the search for freedom in Chekhov and the 'arduous education process through which he strove to attain freedom' (Rahv, 219); similarly, Kepesh talks about 'that sense of personal freedom to which Chekhov is devoted' (*Professor*, 157–8). As an academic Kepesh's interest is in 'licence and restraint in Chekhov's world—longing fulfilled, pleasure denied' (157), which of course reflects his own longings and denials, and his reluctance to be a slave to passion. At the heart of Chekhov's message for Rahv is the fact that 'man can hope to realise the promise of his humanity only if he succeeds in overcoming the slave within himself and in all his guises and disguises' (220); according to him this is the 'moral intuition controlling' Chekhov's work, and Kepesh feels this too, identifying a similar moral struggle taking place in himself. Importantly also, Rahv cites Rilke's poem 'Archaic Torso of Apollo' in his article and argues that the dictum, 'you must change your life,' is implicit in the entire Chekhovian statement' (220). As Alter notes, this is either a huge coincidence, or Roth was inspired to use this poem in *The Breast* as a consequence of reading Rahv's piece on Chekhov, and the article may well have helped him develop his sense of Kepesh's predicament *as* Chekhovian.

There is a degree to which the whole style and tone of *Professor* is Chekhovian. For instance, George Baker's commentating of Chekhov's plays suggests that they are 'never tragic, though they have moments of sorrow and loss' and maintains that, though they have elements of comedy, 'they are not forthrightly comic' (161). Likewise, *Professor,* while marked by moments of regret and loss, could not be considered tragic; and the tone of the novel, though often comic—particularly when relating scenes with Kepesh's parents—is tempered by melancholy and what Stephen Kellman terms 'wistful human scepticism' (30–1). The latter is evident in the book's disinclination to offer answers to Kepesh's problem and its apparent, albeit reluctant conclusion that there aren't any. There is a kind of Chekhovian mingling of comedy and pathos, then, which again seems to draw together or synthesise earlier styles. The tonal balance Roth achieves here has been noted by serval critics: Richard Roth, for instance, describes the tone as a mixture of 'desperate wit and poignant longing' (17), while John Barkham writes perceptively that it is a 'summation of [Roth's] divergent approaches to fiction, a fusing of his earlier styles and themes with his later manner' (1–2). Chekhov provides the perfect complement to Roth's style and preoccupations in this book, then, but Kafka features again here too, and this adds another important element to the story, as will be seen.

Kafka's Whore

Though Kepesh cannot reconcile the professor and the rake, there is a powerful symbol of synthesis to be found in the dream sequence that precedes the final pastoral section. It was shown above how *The Breast* creates a symbol of unity in its central image, and also how Roth constructs a moment of unity for Tarnopol in *My Life as a Man*: the image of the latter in women's clothes unites conformity and dissent, at least in the extent to which they are expressed in gendered terms. A similar function is served in *Professor* via Kepesh's dream of Kafka's whore. There is a sense in which the image of Kafka's whore unifies opposites: Kafka himself signifies restraint in Roth's novel: as Kepesh tells Claire, he maintained that 'the only food fit for a man is half a lemon' (*Professor*, 178); Kafka is viewed as the 'hunger artist' epitome of control and denial, a writer who, to use Martin Greenburg's words, 'doesn't know what pleasure is in art' (*The Terror of Art*, 90). If we associate the idea of a whore with sexual desire, then the image of Kafka's whore becomes an incongruous yoking together of desire and restraint. In this dream sequence Kepesh is introduced to the old lady by Bratasky—the dissenting influence from his boyhood—and this makes it clear that the episode relates to Kepesh's own desires and his own 'hunger artist' struggle not to give in to them. So on a symbolic level Kafka's aging whore represents a unification of the conflicting impulses that fracture Roth's protagonist here.

The dream episode, which itself feels like a parody of Kafka's fiction, comes at a time when Kepesh is ostensibly healthy. At this point he has met Claire and has achieved a kind of moral and emotional equilibrium, feeling 'triumphant: capacious indeed' and, after the disruption and insecurity of his former life, he is finally able to say in Lawrentian style: 'Oh, I have come through' (*Professor*,

186). The old woman, or more specifically the old woman's vagina, becomes a site where antithetical notions combine, and in this respect she is linked to Kepesh's potential happiness: as the guide says to him, 'we only want to make you happy, to make you finally you, David dear,' (192). Presumably this relates to the possibility of Kepesh achieving balance in his life and reconciling his contradictory impulses. However, as a paradoxical representation of both unity and antithesis this symbol is unstable. It is worth recalling how Roland Barthes in *S/Z* discusses antithesis in relation to Balzac's *Sarrasine*, and the incongruous juxtaposition of a Castrato and a young woman; his point about the 'transgression' of antithesis is applicable here:

> Antithesis is a wall without a doorway. Leaping this wall is a transgression. Subject to the antithesis on inside and outside, heat and cold, life and death, the old man and the young woman are separated by the most inflexible barriers: that of meaning. Thus anything that draws these antipathetic sides together is rightly scandalous. (65)

Barthes is writing about the impossibility of overcoming antithesis. He argues that antithesis is a fundamental axiom in a Cartesian sense because it achieves definition through opposition and an 'inflexible barrier' of 'meaning.' The opposition at the heart of *Professor* is also irreconcilable thanks to just such a barrier of meaning: desire and restraint cannot be resolved in Kepesh because they are opposites. As a result, the antithesis expressed symbolically as an old woman's vagina is also 'scandalous' in the manner that Barthes suggests. According to Barthes the yoking together of the Castrato and the young woman in *Sarrasine* 'symbolically…affirms the non-viability of the dual body' (66), and likewise the image of Kafka's whore's vagina suggests the non-viability of the synthesis *it* symbolises, and hence it anticipates the disruption of harmony Kepesh has ostensibly achieved with Claire. Barthes says that when such spurious symbols occur a supplement is produced at the 'site of transgression' that condemns the synthesis to collapse, and the non-viability of the symbol attests to the non-viability of the synthesis: in his words, the symbol is 'damned' (68). The image of Kafka's whore's vagina is grotesque, even repulsive, as suggested by Kepesh's warning: 'Students of literature, you must conquer your squeamishness…you must face the unseemly thing itself' (*Professor*, 191); and this befits the shock associated with the antithetical impasse that Barthes identifies. Also, just as the transgressive juxtaposition of opposites lacks stability in *Sarrasine*, so the symbol of Kafka's whore is unstable and transitory. This is suggested partly because the image occurs in a dream; also the woman is an anarchist's widow and associated with collapse in this sense too. It is significant that Kepesh questions whether or not she is genuine ('I found myself rather doubting the authenticity of the pubic hair' (192)) and that he says 'this woman is nobody' (190). Her instability as a symbol points to the impossibility of the synthesis that she represents and the inevitable breakdown of the harmony he felt he might have achieved with Claire.

So once more this novel, like *The Breast* and *My Life as a Man*, does not, as it were, reify the conformity/dissent conflict; it does not construct it as a fixed hierarchy. It is presented as a dynamic opposition that persists beyond the close of the book. Once more the narrative has an interrogative feel and there is no privileging of duty or dissent. The prose continues to adopt the synthesis of styles seen in *The Breast* and in the 'My True Story' section of *My Life as a Man*—a mingling of high and low styles that might be seen as a stylistic analogue for the amalgam of high and low, sobriety and indulgence, fire and hearth, scholar and rake, that Kepesh wants to achieve in his life.

'The Only Real People are the People Who Never Existed:' The Professor and Postmodernism

Again this novel has the patina of postmodernism, not least because it demonstrates what Peter Brooker calls postmodernism's tendency to 'raid' 'past art' and present 'recycled images' (3). Not only does it ironically reuse styles and tropes from Kafka and Chekhov, but like *My Life as a Man* it exists in ironic relation to Roth's own work in the way it invokes the knowledge of informed Roth readers. As in the previous books, these fictional experiments are quite subtle. It is a long way from the overt experimentation that characterised the first wave of American postmodernism in the 1960s: the work of writers like John Barth, Richard Brautigan, and Thomas Pynchon, for instance, is marked by the extreme black comedy that Roth himself employed in *Portnoy, Our Gang,* and *The Great American Novel.* The overt comedy and experimentation associated with 1960s postmodernism isn't a part of Roth's aesthetic here: the style Roth introduces with *The Breast* remains subtly ironic; both works are clearly self-conscious but there is an element of restraint throughout, so much so that ostensibly there seems little to distinguish them from conventional realism. It is indicative perhaps of the 'elusive and ironic realism' that Malcolm Bradbury identified as having emerged in 1970s American fiction as 'the handy Sixties distinction between realism and experiment grows ever less credible' (267–8). According to Bradbury, a form of 'neo-realism' characterised American writing throughout the 70s and 80s that is 'rarely a realism of felt authenticity, nor moral humanism' (272). Again this illustrates a point that John Mepham made about postmodernism in the early 1990s:

> In our time, postmodernism is not the anti-mimetic experimentalism of the obscurantists, but the pleasurably ironic return to fictional forms of coherent storytelling. (153)

Indeed, far from being 'anti-mimetic,' some have argued that Roth makes a case for the referential nature of literature in *Professor.* Alice Kaminsky, for instance, suggests that the book is actually about mimesis in literature, and works to support anti-postmodernist/ poststructuralist views:

> What Kepesh experiences as a man and what he reads as a lover of literature are inextricably related; one activity reinforces that other in a reciprocal sustaining relationship. (53)

Referring to the lecture he drafts for Literature 341, she writes that 'Kepesh clearly rejects the 'new novel' theory of fiction; for him fiction is referential;' and she concludes by suggesting that

> Oscar Wilde's famous and perverse witticism…that in art 'the only real people are the people who never existed,' is given a different twist by Roth who believes that the 'reality principle' involves people in books who 'refer' to people who exist.

In effect, through Kepesh, Roth becomes the 'Defender of the Faith,' the faith of literary realism. (54)

It is certainly the case that life and literature have a symbiotic relationship in this novel. Life comes to resemble Chekhovian art in the pastoral scene, for example, and Kepesh is forever trying to understand his life through his reading. Indeed, Roth himself champions an approach to reading that focuses on this relationship, and he sounds a lot like Kepesh in one interview where he suggests that as a teacher he forbids 'on pain of expulsion' the words 'structure, form and symbol' in the classroom, in order to improve the students' 'thinking.' However, the referential/non-referential debate does not interest him in a theoretical sense, as he states explicitly: 'As for structuralism: it hasn't played any part in my life. I'm afraid I can't satisfy you [the interviewer] with a vituperative denunciation ('Interview *with Le Nouvel Observateur*' in *Reading Myself*, 120). The issue of the relationship between art and life has concerned Roth a good deal, of course, both as a novelist and as a critic; indeed, throughout the late 1970s, 80s and 90s it is central to his work. It is also a subject that features in many of the interviews and essays collected in *Reading Myself and Others*, and it is worth citing the author's note to the 1985 edition of that collection:

> Together these pieces reveal to me a continuing preoccupation with the relationship between the written and unwritten world. This simple distinction (embracing a complex phenomenon) is borrowed from Paul Goodman. I find it more useful than the distinction between imagination and reality, or art and life, first, because everyone can think through readily enough to the clear-cut differences between the two, and second, because the worlds that I feel myself shuttling between everyday couldn't be more succinctly described. Back and forth, back and forth, bearing fresh information, detailed instructions, garbled messages, desperate enquiries, naïve expectations, baffling challenges…in all, cast somewhat in the role of the courier Barnabas, whom the Land Surveyor K. enlists to traverse the steep winding road between the village and the castle in Kafka's novel about the difficulties of getting through. (ix/x)

It is interesting, and typical, that Roth is keen to complicate what some may mistake for a 'simple distinction,' likening himself to Kafka's Barnabas moving between the unfathomable Klamm and the perpetually bewildered K. Evidently Roth agrees with Paul Goodman that it is a 'complex phenomenon,' that there are some differences between the 'written' and the 'unwritten' that, like the mysteries of Kafka's Castle, are not, and will never be 'clear cut'; the implication is that the two do indeed overlap in complicated and significant ways. We will see how interesting these issues become when Roth himself takes centre stage as his own protagonist later in his career. Here it is sufficient to note how his public statements complicating the distinction between the 'written' and 'unwritten' implicate him in his fiction, foregrounding authorial presence as an issue, and constructing it as something to speculate about, and to be uncertain about, in his writing.

Roth's writing remains obviously aware of itself, then, and most importantly it continues to exhibit the uncertainty that one associates with postmodernism: the point of wisdom discernible in the earlier texts remains elusive, and this continues to be the case in his later writing. Also the self-conscious/self-reflexive feel of Roth's fiction qualifies any sense we might have of Roth's writing as realism at this stage: when art reflects life in the pastoral scenes of *Professor* this augments our sense of the fictiveness of the scene and confounds any simple notion we might have about the relationship between fiction and reality, both in relation to Kepesh's life, and our own. Irony and the uncertainty become dominant in his writing in the mid-70s, and this persists in the work that follows, as does the focus on the Rothian dilemma.

The Self I Ought to Be: *Zuckerman Bound*

Though Zuckerman as a character first features in *My Life as a Man,* the Zuckerman books proper begin with *The Ghost Writer* in 1979. This is the novel in which Roth first begins to use Zuckerman as a kind of fictional surrogate or alter-ego. Essentially Zuckerman's life resembles Roth's own; he was born in Newark, became a writer whose work upset the Jewish community, published a controversial bestseller that made him famous, and then has to deal with the consequences. Throughout the Zuckerman books Roth uses this character partly to explore and interrogate the artistic, emotional and ethical issues that his own early writing raised. What does it mean to write confessional fiction? To what extent is it legitimate to do so? What moral obligations, if any, does a writer of such material have? And so on.

Higher Education: The Ghost Writer

In *The Ghost Writer* Nathan Zuckerman is a young writer who goes to visit his literary hero, an old writer called Lonoff. Nathan has just published a short story, 'Higher Education,' that has upset his father, in a similar way that some of Roth's early stories upset the Jewish community. The story takes a family episode as its subject, upsetting his father because he thinks it's a misrepresentation of the family: 'there's more to the family…than is in this story' he says, and he worries that it presents Jewish people in a bad light: 'what will the Gentiles think?' (87; 92)[1] Nathan argues that he has written

---

1   Four Zuckerman books: *The Ghost Writer, Zuckerman Unbound, The Anatomy Lesson,* and *The Prague Orgy* were published as one volume, *Zuckerman Bound* (New York: Farrar, Straus, Giroux, 1985). *The Ghost Writer* was first published 1979, *Zuckerman Unbound* in 1981, *The Anatomy Lesson* 1983, and *The Prague Orgy* in 1985. All future page references will be made to the collected edition.

a piece of art and so can't be shackled by concerns about fidelity to the lived experience; also, as an artist, he can't be constrained by the sensitivities of those who might be upset by his art. His father's response is 'People don't read art—they read about people. And they judge them as such' (92). When people read his story, he says, they'll be reading principally about Jewish people's so-called love of money. So here the Rothian dilemma takes the form of how to reconcile Zuckerman's artistic integrity with the expectations of his father: the desire to indulge his creative life is set against the duty he feels to family and the community in general.

Zuckerman, like Kepesh, has a father to please, then, and the words used to chastise Zuckerman are reminiscent of those employed by Kepesh's father in *Professor*. Recall, for instance, the scene when the mysterious caller harasses Kepesh at his apartment in the middle of the night. It comes following Kepesh's breakdown, and his father berates him for the mess he seems to be making of his life: he is anxious because Kepesh is seeing a psychiatrist, taking antidepressants, and apparently associating with dubious folk: '"All this is *wrong*, son. It is no way to live! A psychiatrist and being on strong drugs, and people showing up at all hours—people who aren't even people"' (*Professor*, 114–5). When Kepesh pleads with his father not make too much of it, he answers, 'And don't you make so little' (116). And of course he is right: Kepesh's father offers a 'common sense' assessment of his son's predicament and makes the important point—albeit in a comically backhanded way—that there is no such thing as people who don't matter. While his father might be said to be overreacting to the mysterious caller, there is also a possibility that this man *could* be a threat to his son's safety, and to deny that is reckless. Indeed, while Kepesh might feel irritated by his father's fussiness and naivety, he also feels the force of his point, as evidenced by the fact that he can never fully embrace the reckless facet of own his character. Nathan's father sounds very similar to Kepesh's and makes a related 'common sense' point when he tells his son that, 'People...read about people.' In other words, when it comes to people—whether they're ringing your doorbell, reading your stories (or appearing in them)—everything potentially matters.

And while Zuckerman, like Kepesh, is exasperated by his father's views, he too eventually realizes that the old man has a point.

Zuckerman meets a young woman at Lonoff's house called Amy Bellete, who he begins to fantasize is Anne Frank: in his imagination she has survived the Holocaust and is now living under an assumed name in America. Zuckerman's Anne Frank doesn't reveal her identity either to the public or to her father Otto because to do so would be to compromise the impact of her diary. If it was known she was alive it would reduce the book to just another teenager's diary: it has much more power if readers believe that she is dead; likewise, if readers met the real Anne she'd never match the myth they've made of her. So in a sense she sacrifices her father's happiness for the sake of the diary; art takes precedence over filial responsibility and, from Nathan's perspective, this offers a justification for the decision to continue writing what he wants, despite his father. Importantly Zuckerman imagines having a relationship with Anne Frank and introducing her to his family: he feels that being linked with a Jewish heroine would help redeem him in his parents' eyes, making him heroic by association. This fantasy serves a similar function to other fantasies in Roth's writing, attempting to unite conflicting aspects of the hero's psyche. Zuckerman creates an adult Anne and in this way expresses himself as an artist, indulging himself in the activity that has made him a transgressor; but at the same time the fiction he creates symbolically reconciles him with the community from which he is estranged. Like Tarnopol the cross-dresser, and Kepesh the creator of Kafka's whore, Zuckerman's imagination unites the antithesis that torments him (conformity/dissent). But again this middle ground of the imagination is an unstable union, as its status as a figment of Nathan's imagination attests.

Roth also uses this reincarnated Anne Frank to make an important point about writing. At one point, for instance, Anne is shown reflecting on her diary, astonished at the lack of resemblance between how she is and how she appears in her narrative ('I view the affairs of a certain 'Anne'…as if she were a stranger' (135)); also, as suggested, she is astonished by the difference between her sense of her own character, and the Anne that people have created as a consequence of reading her book: she says that the public's 'Anne Frank is theirs ... Child Martyr and Holy Saint.... They wouldn't have me, not as I am' (154); there would be a disparity between Anne the icon and the Anne of reality. The point is that the writing 'I' is always a fiction: both the act of reading and that of writing inevitably distort it. This demonstrates the naivety of Nathan's and his father's views of fiction. While the latter is naïve for imagining that writing reflects any kind of truth about the world, or that it's possible to tell the whole story; the former is naïve for assuming that his own writing will be interpreted in line with his intentions, and that it doesn't have consequences. While people in stories clearly *aren't* people, people *still* read about people.

Instead of constructing the dissenting Zuckerman as superior to his detractors (represented here by his father), then, Roth reveals him to be just as naïve as his critics. In other words, in keeping with the spirit of uncertainty introduced with Kepesh, there is no point of wisdom in this story either. The style of the novel is also reminiscent of the Kepesh books. *The Ghost Writer* has a humorous tone, but this is not the result of caricature, as is the case in Portnoy; rather Nathan's voice has a self-mocking quality: he narrates his story from a point twenty years in the future and humour is often derived from his own ironic perception of his former naivety and earnestness. Where Portnoy's detractors are ridiculed by the narrator and their opinion diminished, here, as in *The Breast* and *Professor*, the narrator's attitude is infinitely more respectful and sympathetic. Consider how movingly Nathan describes his father following one of their arguments:

> What I saw, when I turned to wave goodbye for the winter, was my smallish, smartly dressed father—turned out for my visit in a new 'fingertip' car coat ... what I saw was my bewildered father, alone on the darkening street corner by the park that used to be our paradise, thinking himself and all of the Jewry gratuitously disgraced and jeopardized by my inexplicable betrayal. (95–6)

Quite a few critics saw the book as an apology of sorts for the extreme views associated with Roth's earlier writing; Anatole Broyard, for instance, suggested that 'it is almost as if the author of *Portnoy's Complaint* owes us a debt of inhibition' (13). Readings of this kind attest to how Roth has tempered the expression of the Rothian dilemma since Portnoy, and how the balanced, interrogative voices of Kepesh and Tarnopol persist in the first of Roth's Zuckerman novels.

Cutthroat Caricaturist: Zuckerman Unbound

Roth ups the ante for his authorial surrogate in the next Zuckerman book, *Zuckerman Unbound* (1982). In this novel Zuckerman has published *Carnovsky*, which can be seen as the fictional version of *Portnoy's Complaint*, and is having to deal with the consequences of celebrity, and, not least, the vitriol of the Jewish community who accuse him of anti-Semitism. Worse, Zuckerman's writing has distanced him still further from his family, so much so that Zuckerman's calls his son a 'bastard' on his deathbed. In other words, after the publication of his bestseller, Zuckerman's problems increase with the size of his audience.

Still the Rothian dilemma persists, and again Zuckerman's problem looks a lot like Kepesh's. Like Kepesh, Zuckerman is torn between the fireside and the furnace. On the one hand he craves an ordered and respectable life; he attempts to achieve this through a relationship with an extremely respectable woman called Laura: she is 'generous, devoted, thoughtful, kindhearted' (*Zuckerman Bound*, 231) and plays a similar role to Claire in *Professor*. Laura is a benign female presence who acts as a palliative for the hero after a period of domestic turbulence: as she says at one stage, 'After the … wives … I was just perfect…. No tears, no fits…. You could get your work done with me' (341). This relationship is unstable because, like Kepesh, Zuckerman has a darker side that is crucial to his character and his creative life. He cannot reconcile the aspect of himself that would be an acceptable partner for Laura, with his status as—to use Zuckerman's own words—a 'cutthroat caricaturist' and the 'coldhearted betrayer of the most intimate confessions' (234); as a consequence, their relationship is 'subvert[ed] by everything that enlivens [his] writing' (235) and he begins to find the relationship 'boring' (341). His ambivalence toward Laura recalls Kepesh's ambivalence toward Claire, of course, and once more the protagonist's dueling impulses preclude the possibility of contentment. Thus while his agent is right to observe that 'there's a little mother superior' in Zuckerman (257), ultimately, like Kepesh, he concludes that 'the virtue racket ill becomes' him (234). In his relationship with Laura the conformity/ dissent dichotomy is again expressed in obvious terms: she stands for an ordered, conventional life, but the hero cannot commit if he is to be true to his own instincts and desires. Once more this text retains the interrogative feel and balanced tone of the Kepesh books; certainly Roth presents Zuckerman's relationship with Laura in such a way as not to condemn either party. As in *Portnoy's Complaint*, a number of the hero's detractors—i.e. society's representatives—are given voice in the novel, but as in Roth's interrogative fictions this novel allows those voices an equal degree of force to the hero's. Laura's case against Zuckerman, for instance, is strongly articulated by Rosemary. She implies that Zuckerman is Laura's moral inferior and attacks him for hurting that 'wonderful girl' (350); and even as Zuckerman defends himself he is shown to be feeling the force of her condemnation; indeed, with regard to Laura, the case against Zuckerman is put partly by himself ('How could you *not* love…Laura? How could *he* not? (231)). When the argument about Laura concludes both parties— Zuckerman and Rosemary—are equally criticized: while Zuckerman shows Rosemary to be stupid for naively conflating his real life with his character ('confusing the dictating ventriloquist with the demonic dummy' (348), he concedes that *he* is 'stupid' for imagining that he 'had done absolutely nothing to harm Laura' (350). In other words, the world is not absolutely wrong and Zuckerman is not absolutely right. Thus while the desire/duty dilemma features as strongly as ever, it is again presented in a non-hierarchical way. In general Roth seems less sure of himself and hence less willing to endorse either individual or consensus values: the old dilemma persists for his hero, and in this sense life hasn't changed, just faith in an ability to fathom it. We get the impression that the writer of these novels has opinions, but he is uncertain of their ultimate value or viability.

The Experience of Contradiction: The Anatomy Lesson

Zuckerman's dilemma is made physically manifest in *The Anatomy Lesson*, where the hero finds himself prostrate with a crippling back complaint which—as with Kepesh's metamorphosis—may or may not be a symptom of his various anxieties. In this third book his authorial guilt has been compounded: where earlier Zuckerman's father called him a bastard on his deathbed, here his mother dies, but not before writing the word 'Holocaust' on a sheet of paper; such is the significance of this that Zuckerman can't let it go, carrying it around with him in his pocket. This obviously adds more weight to Zuckerman's sense of being an apostate son, and so-called betrayer of the Jewish community. By now he has reached his physical and emotional nadir, but while he feels he is 'too delicate by far for [his] own contradictions' (644), those contradictions persist, as does Roth's interrogative approach to expressing them: thus while Zuckerman contemplates whether or not he is guilty of 'punish[ing] his adoring mother … behind the mask of fiction,' he tells us that, in 'a school debate,' he 'could have argued persuasively for either proposition' (474). Similarly, when Zuckerman is attacked by a critic who questions the ultimate worth of his fiction, he responds by conceding that the critic might be right. Interestingly this attack resembles one made by the distinguished critic Irving Howe after the publication of *Portnoy's Complaint*: in *The Anatomy Lesson* Howe is reincarnated as a fictional critic, Milton Appel,[1] but while Zuckerman refers to Appel as a 'bastard' and an 'idiot,' he ultimately concedes that 'even the worst criticism contains some truth,' and wonders, 'How do I even know that Appel isn't right?' (507). Again it is very hard to miss the lengths Roth is going to in order to achieve an equally weighted representation of Zuckerman's moral status.

Throughout the cycle Zuckerman often thinks of himself as a performer, adopting different roles in different contexts, and this trait features heavily in the third installment. It will be recalled that occasionally Kepesh is presented in this way too: sometimes this is

---

1   Many critics have seen the parallels here, see for instance Lawrence E. Mintz, 'Devil and Angel: Philip Roth's Humour,' 162.

explicitly the case—as when he is a character in his own dream, and sometimes it is implicit, as in the Chekhovian pastoral scenes at the end of *Professor*. Occasionally this notion of performance is more fundamental and relates to his conception of character. As young man, for instance, we saw that Kepesh shied away from acting because it was too frivolous, but even as he did so he conceded that there may not be a real self to draw on: 'At twenty I must stop impersonating others and Become Myself, or at least begin to impersonate the self I believe I ought to be now' (*Professor*, 12). In *The Anatomy Lesson* Zuckerman becomes a performer too, imagining different identities in order to express different aspects of his personality: most notably he imagines himself as a doctor, on the one hand, and a pornographer on the other. For a man with Zuckerman's background, a job as a doctor represents the quintessential conformist profession: it is a profession that would have pleased his parents, enabling his transition from 'filial outcast to Jewish internist' (*Zuckerman Bound*, 587); like marrying Anne Frank, it would redeem him in the eyes of his parents, as well as with the critics who abhor his fiction: at one point, for instance, he tells us that he 'owed' a career in gynecology 'to women after *Carnovsky*' (577); thus, while writing is 'not a very sociable business' for Zuckerman, a career as a pediatrician would redeem him socially and morally: it would offer him the opportunity to go 'back to school and the days of effortlessly satisfying the powers that be' (645). Roth offsets this by having Zuckerman pose as a pornographer and editor of a magazine called *Lickety Split*. While as a doctor Zuckerman constructs himself as a social being, as a pornographer he is markedly *anti*social and 'will never be the good acceptable Jew, never' (625); as a doctor he could atone for demeaning women in his novels, as a pornographer he becomes misogynistic, particularly to those he calls 'those fucking fascistic feminists' (628). The conflicting aspects of Zuckerman's personality are clearly expressed here then: doctor versus pornographer, which again equates in an obvious way to Kepesh as a professor of desire and his dual roles as scholar and rake. Zuckerman's moral and emotional schizophrenia is at odds with society's demand for psychological integration, but he responds, not like Kepesh with a retreat from the Symbolic Order, but by imagining two antithetical social roles for himself. These roles become an expression of a need for unity, but it is a unity that Zuckerman understands is not only untenable but, in a sense, undesirable. At this stage he has come to understand that contradiction is not only inevitable, but fundamental to the human condition: as he says explicitly at one stage, 'The experience of contradiction *is* the human experience' (644). Indeed, the more Zuckerman reflects on his own dueling impulses the more he realizes that this is what makes him a novelist.

> The doctors are all confidence; the pornographers are all con-
> fidence … while doubt is half a writer's life. Two thirds. Nine
> tenths. Another day, another doubt. The only thing I never
> doubted was the doubt. (674)

He turns the conflict that fractures his character into a justifica-
tion for his vocation: this is *why* he is a novelist, and he couldn't and indeed shouldn't be a novelist without it. 'A novelist without his irreconcilable halves [is] someone who hasn't the means to make novels. Nor the right' (645). The implication is that people who are convinced by the validity of their own arguments should write politi-
cal manifestos, not novels. Perhaps this is an insight that only the hero as artist can make: certainly Kepesh—the hero as critic—struggled to see his conflict of 'irreconcilable halves' as anything other than a negative thing. There is a degree of acceptance in Zuckerman as he voices the philosophy that seems to underpin everything Roth writes following *The Breast*. From that point all of his writing seems intent on acknowledging doubt, and achieving parity in the way irreconcilable halves are conveyed. Indeed, in the late interview in which he announced his retirement he reiterates the extent to which doubt has informed his writing life, and it appears to be one of the reasons he has decided to abandon it:

> Writing means always being wrong. All your drafts tell the story
> of your failures. I don't have the energy of frustration anymore,
> or the strength to confront myself. Because to write is to be frus-
> trated. You spend your time writing the wrong word, the wrong
> sentence, the wrong story. You continually fool yourself, you

continually fail, and so you have to live in a state of perpetual frustration. You spend your time telling yourself, That doesn't work, I have to start again. Oh, that doesn't work either—and you start again. I'm tired of all that work. (Nelly Kaprielian, unpaginated)

This suggests that to make art out of doubt one needs to care about the struggle; the compulsion to seek solutions in the face of their perpetual absence is a requirement and a constant frustration for as long as one is content to call oneself an artist.

A Storytelling Son: The Prague Orgy

The drive to conform is still strong in Zuckerman of course, as seen in his desire to become a pediatrician: the mature Zuckerman wants to please his dead father as much as Kepesh wanted to please *his* father, and this continues in *The Prague Orgy*, the so-called epilogue of *Zuckerman Bound*. In this novella-length work Zuckerman wants to make up for his transgressions as a Jewish writer by travelling to Prague in order to save the manuscripts of an obscure Jewish writer. In this way Zuckerman will be making his father proud by doing something positive for Jewish culture: in one sense this is a quest for moral salvation and Jewish credibility. Again this works as a symbol of unity, in a similar way to Kepesh's status as a breast, the image of Kafka's whore, the idea of Zuckerman as Anne Frank's lover, and as a doctor/pornographer. As a saviour of Jewish art Zuckerman can maintain his dissenting profession as a writer, whilst simultaneously play the role of moral being. His irreconcilable halves are reconciled. However, this ambition is exposed and ridiculed in the novel; as Olga says to Zuckerman at one point:

> O. So that's what you get out of it! That's your idealism! The marvellous Zuckerman brings from behind the iron curtain two hundred unpublished Yiddish stories written by a victim of a Nazi bullet. You will be a hero to the Jews and to literature and to all the free world. (770)

Indeed, Zuckerman himself is self-aware enough to begin to see through his mission, coming to suspect that his task is indeed a performance of atonement:

> Is this a passionate struggle for those marvellous stories or a renewal of the struggle toward self-caricature? Still the son, still the child in strenuous pursuit of the father's loving response? (766)

There are references to performance throughout this epilogue that underscore the sense we have of Zuckerman's mission as an ironic, constructed activity; indeed, in parts the narrative actually takes the form of a play, with scenes presented in dramatic dialogue. In this way the narrative foregrounds its own artifice, signaling representation as a performance of representation, creating an ironic frame for the ironic author-hero. This has been the case throughout the trilogy, but this epilogue goes further, acknowledging the extent to which *everything* is a construction: including the idea of origin and meaning. As well as via the constant references to artifice and performance, this point is made in the way the book deals with fathers and father figures. All of the father figures in *The Prague Orgy* are seen as having been fictionalised to some degree: as one critic observed when discussing this book, 'fathers, even Kafka's father, are filial constructions'(174). In an earlier incarnation Zuckerman pondered 'the fiction [he] made of [his] father' (*Zuckerman Bound*, 379), and in the epilogue too his father is perceived as an invention. Similarly, according to Zuckerman, Novak—the Minister for Culture—has invented *his* father; he refers to him as 'another character out of mock-autobiography, yet another fabricated father manufactured to serve the purpose of a storytelling son' (*Zuckerman Bound*, 783). Worst of all, the son of the author of the stories Zuckerman strives to rescue, Sisovsky, has also invented his father, as Zuckerman realises when he learns that he was run over by a bus and not, as Sisovsky claims, killed by a Nazi bullet. This idea of the fictionalised father is particularly interesting in relation to the question of writing, and Roth's postmodernism. As readers we cannot help but make connections with the notion of truth and origin, but *The Prague Orgy* underscores what might be called a poststructuralist conception of origin. Derrida suggested that the 'specificity of writing [is] intimately bound up to the absence of the father,' implying that absence rather than presence gives rise to meaning' (quoted in Brenda Marshall, 122). All the fathers in *The Prague Orgy* are absent in the sense that they are unknowable in their true essence—all the sons can offer are reconstructions that serve their own purposes. The absence of a definable origin of meaning is significant of course: if it is the sons who make meaning here, then what is its value? How does one relate to the past morally if that relationship is merely a construction?

Just like Kepesh at the end of *Professor*, then, Zuckerman here can only conceive of his life in terms of art and artifice: for Kepesh the critic, this took the form of the Chekhov stories that fuel his literary scholarship; for Zuckerman the novelist it is his *own* equally spurious constructions that seem to come between him and reality. And just as Kepesh can only impersonate the self he 'ought to be,' so Zuckerman can only impersonate the selves that he feels that *he* ought to be, such as 'hero to the Jews.' But this novella seems to go further by confirming what was only implied in *Professor*: because reality is inaccessible, impersonation is all that is available.

Pastorals and Benign Females Revisited

We saw that Claire Ovington represents the quintessential benign female for Kepesh; she epitomises a certain type of female character who features again in the shape of Laura in *Zuckerman Unbound*. In Roth's scheme such females are nurturing, sensible, and loving, offering the possibility of a stable and ordered life for the protagonist. They are associated with a potential life of pastoral contentment, as in the final scenes of *Professor* when Kepesh rents a farm for the summer with Claire: 'A small, two-storied white clapboard farmhouse…set halfway up a hillside of dandelions and daisies from a silent, untraveled road.' With its 'gentle green hills and distant green mountains' this takes Kepesh back to his childhood, providing a sense of 'living at last in accordance with my true spirit, that, indeed, I am "home"' (*Professor*, 196). The allure of such women is ambivalent, of course, as Kepesh's ex-wife Helen discerns when she visits them in their ostensible idyll: while Claire represents 'common sense' (158) for Kepesh, Helen wonders whether 'reason and common sense are what [he] need[s]' (95). Similarly, we saw how Zuckerman—while appreciative of Laura's qualities—finds it impossible to reconcile himself to a life with her. A comparable benign female features in the form of Maria Freshfield in *The Counterlife* (1986), and again in the so-called Roth books, *The Facts* (1989) and *Deception* (1990). Like Kepesh's Claire, Maria represents much that the dissenting Roth hero aspires to: a calm life with a caring and level-headed woman. As a middle class English woman in *The Counterlife*, Maria is also associated with a kind of pastoral idyll for the Roth hero, this time represented by England and Englishness. As will be seen, England comes to represent a potential sanctuary for the beleaguered Zuckerman; it is an alternative, seemingly tranquil environment akin in many ways to the Sullivan County farmhouse where Kepesh dreams of quiet and happy life. This section will explore the representation of England and Englishness in Roth's writing in order to consider the bearing it has on the significance of the pastoral in his work, and its relationship with what we have termed the Rothian dilemma.

Roth's England

Over the first forty years of his career, Roth showed himself to be something of a contemporary Henry James: a New World son with an Old World sensibility. For many years he was romantically involved with the English actress Claire Bloom—principally the eighties and early nineties—and he divided his time between homes in the US and the UK; thus like James he was well placed to compare and contrast English and American culture. In many respects he appeared to be something of an anglophile. As we have seen, again like James, some of Roth's work belongs in what Philip Rahv termed the 'paleface' tradition of American writing: his aesthetic models are occasionally European and he has often displayed an orientation toward European, and particularly English, notions of literary refinement and sophistication.

It will be recalled too that Kepesh goes to England to study as a graduate student, and while he is upset not to find himself living in King's College's Bloomsbury accommodation, London soon redeems itself in his eyes when it provides him with his first ever sexual encounter with a prostitute, an unequivocally positive experience for Kepesh. In this early portrait London is shown to be rich with cultural diversity: along with the exotic Elisabeth and Birgitta, Kepesh encounters Indians and Africans on the Earl's Court Road. As Roth's career developed, however, the author begins to display a less positive view of England, comparing what he sees as the stifling cultural homogeneity of England with the plurality and eclecticism of America. For instance, in interview with Jonathan Brent in 1988 Roth said:

> Try to imagine England inviting, on the scale that the US does, the cultural and political clashes—and, above all, the linguistic and racial 'impurities'—that are the inevitable consequence of permitting millions and millions of foreigners alien to the main-

stream society, language and heritage to settle into one's developed country year in and year out. The wholesale colonisation of England's major cities by third world immigrants ... is unthinkable. (230–6)

This is at odds with Kepesh's portrait of London's ethnic mix a decade earlier. Indeed, as far as Roth is concerned, racism is endemic in English society and culture. In the later novel, *Deception* (1990), for instance, his protagonist, Philip (who we're meant to see as an incarnation of Roth himself) describes his shock at an advertisement for cigarillos he sees on English TV:

> It showed the final moments of a performance of a play featuring Dickens's Fagin, a Fagin complete with enormous hooked nose and dishevelled mop of greasy hair. The curtain comes down, Fagin takes his bows - and then the actor is back in his dressing gown, in of his mirror pulling off his hooked nose and the ugly wig and scrubbing himself back to normal with cold cream. Underneath the makeup there is, lo and behold, a fair-haired, handsome, youngish middle-aged, rather upper-class English actor. To relax after the performance, he lights up one of these cigarillos, contentedly he puffs away at it, talking about the flavour and the aroma and so on, and then He leans very intimately into the camera and holds up the cigarillo and suddenly, in a thick, Faginy, Yiddish accent and with insinuating leer on his face, he says, 'And best of all, they're cheap. (119–20)

This is his hero's first real exposure to the casual racism of English popular culture—he is so shocked by it that he phones an English Jewish friend explaining what he has just seen: the friend replies, 'Don't worry ... you'll get used to it.' What also troubles Roth is English people's unwillingness to acknowledge that xenophobia exists in English society. Again in *Deception* his protagonist describes being the victim of a verbal racist attack on the streets of London. When, later, he gives an account of this to some English friends they all claim that he is exaggerating the significance of the event:

> they all just laughed and explained to me ... how nuts I am and ... I never felt more misplaced in *any* country than I did listening

to all those intelligent and decent people going on denying what was staring them right in the face. (*Deception*, 105–10)

For Roth in the late 80s and 90s, then, English society is parochial, anti-Semitic, and in denial; the English appear to be cultural dinosaurs. Roth draws attention to all of these characteristics in *The Counterlife*.

'The Heavy Hand of Human Values:' The Counterlife

Before going on to discuss the representation of Englishness in *The Counterlife* it is important to say something about its structure. The experience of reading *The Counterlife* is quite disorientating in that it offers different versions of events, contradicting itself at several stages in the narrative. This happens because the book juxtaposes two ontological levels: a level of fiction and a level of what might be called 'fictional reality.' Chapters 1, 2, 3 and 5 of the novel are a collection of stories featuring Nathan Zuckerman; chapter 4, meanwhile, presents Nathan Zuckerman as their author. In other words, chapter 4 offers a 'fictional reality'—a different level of diegesis or ontological plane in which Nathan Zuckerman supposedly *wrote* his fictions. This ontological hierarchy is quite important as will be seen but, firstly, it is worth discussing what happens in Zuckerman's fictions. Zuckerman's stories are about conflict: the first three, 'Basel', 'Judea' and 'Aloft'—chapters 1, 2 and 3 respectively—are largely concerned with the ideological conflict at the heart of Israeli politics; Zuckerman's final story in chapter 5, 'Christendom,' is about the conflict experienced by Zuckerman himself when he tries to set up home with Maria Freshfield in Chiswick, England.

Let us take the Israeli conflict first. In 'Judea,' Nathan Zuckerman's brother, Henry, after almost dying from surgery, abandons America and his wife and children to follow the Zionist cause in Israel. Nathan goes to Israel to see if he can talk sense into Henry and the story essentially becomes an account of Zuckerman's impression of Israel and its ideological struggles. In this section Roth—in keeping with his determined interrogative strategy and insistence on balance— goes to considerable trouble to present both sides of the ideological rift. Thus Roth has Zuckerman talk to a host Jews with diverse political opinions. As John Updike puts it in his review of the novel, Zuckerman 'talks with disillusioned, almost anti-Israeli Jews, with rabid expansionist Jews, with Jews as crazy as those he meets in New York,' and so on ('Wrestling to be Born,' 107–8). The extreme right and left of the debate is expressed through the characters Mordocai Lippman, an ardent Zionist, on the one hand, and Shuki Elchanan, a liberal journalist, on the other. These two characters 'embody the contemporary conflict between the Israeli Hawk and Dove' (Bonnie Lyons, 186–95). Both are allowed to voice their various positions extensively: each is given the opportunity to deliver his own point of view along with fairly long denunciations of the other. Thus, on the one hand, Shuki tells Zuckerman that he smells 'fascism on people like Lippmann;' while, on the other hand, Lippman tells him that Shuki 'lives in a Middle East that, most unfortunately, does not exist' (*The Counterlife*, 177). There is a real sense in which Roth pitches argument against counter-argument and no closure or resolution of the debate is offered. The various points of view are presented to Zuckerman who, as the focaliser of these narratives, occupies a position at the evaluative centre of the arguments. Zuckerman offers appraisals of the various points of view, adopting a position of tolerance and relative detachment himself: in short he makes an effort to show that he can appreciate both sides of the debate. Thus Zuckerman argues against Lippman and what he calls the 'dogmatic Zionist challenge' (147) but, at the same time, wonders if he is rejecting him 'because what he says is wrong or because what he says is unsayable' (145). He displays the kind of balanced approach to argument that first became a feature of Roth's work in *The Breast*, then: Roth incorporates arguments for the right and the left into his narrative and has Zuckerman tread a tightrope of 'tolerance' between the two. Zuckerman, who is depicted as being rather blasé about his own Jewishness, adopts the position of enlightened, secular and sophisticated writer. This is, of course, still *a position* and, one might conceivably argue, it's potentially the most dangerous of all positions. It is ostensibly the rational, mediating position, offering the voice of reason, yet it is seen by the people involved in the debate as the position of an outsider who views arguments in abstraction.

Indeed, Zuckerman is seen to impose his outsider's 'sophistication' and tolerance on arguments he does not really appreciate. Shuki, for instance, begs Zuckerman not to use his experiences in Israel as material for fiction because, in his view, he does not really understand the country. Shuki tells him that the ideological arguments are 'too damn complicated' to be treated in fiction. Shuki fears that Zuckerman would 'misinterpret everything' because he is 'inclined to be funny and ironical about things one is supposed to be either *for* or *against*' (161–2). When we reach chapter 4, however, we discover that Zuckerman has done exactly what Shuki asked him not to do.

Chapter 4, as suggested above, presents another level of diegesis which reveals that we have been reading Zuckerman's *fictional* account of Israeli politics all along. We discover that Nathan Zuckerman is actually dead and that the initial chapters of the novel were a series of fictions produced by him before his demise. These fictions are discovered by Zuckerman's brother, Henry, who has not become a religious fanatic after all. Readers thought they were reading Zuckerman's life, when really they were reading Zuckerman's art. In *The Counterlife*, then, art and life, what Linda Hutcheon calls 'that familiar humanist separation,' is disrupted and problematized. The art and life distinction also stands, as Hutcheon again has written, for the separation of 'the human imagination and order' on the one hand, 'versus chaos and disorder' on the other (*A Poetics of Postmodernism*, 7). In *The Counterlife* the boundary between art and life collapses and the 'order' that the fictional author (Zuckerman) has attempted to impose on the 'disorder' of 'life' is revealed. This reminds us that the ostensibly balanced account of the Israeli ideological conflict we have just been offered is merely one author's attempt to confine multifarious and irreconcilable arguments within the externally imposed parameters of his subjective reason and rationality. *The Counterlife* cleverly resists such authorial totalizing by exposing it. Zuckerman is revealed as the godlike creator of an artificial world in which complex arguments have been organised by, and inevitably subordinated to, a monologizing single perspective. This novel, in short, strives to expose the folly of trying to express and contain issues that are, to use Shuki's words, 'too damn complicated' for fiction.

So how does this relate to the English and to Roth's perception of Englishness? As suggested, the final chapter of the novel, 'Christendom,' is also one of Zuckerman's fictions. The only difference here is that we know 'Christendom' is fictional before we start to read it: we know that we are being shown another of the dead Zuckerman's stories. In this chapter Zuckerman imagines himself married to the upper-middle class woman Maria Freshfield who is seemingly the quintessential English rose. He describes her as 'a child of the English landless gentry, country reared, Oxford educated ... the embodiment of a cultural background markedly different from my own.'[1] Maria has an anti-Semitic mother and an even more anti-Semitic sister. Her sister, Sarah, tells Zuckerman at one point that

> Maria ought to have told you that she is from the kind of people who, if you knew anything about English society you would have *expected* to be anti-Semitic.... I recommend you [read] Trollope.... It may knock some of the stuffing out of your yearning to partake of English civility. It will tell you all about people like us. Read *The Way We Live Now.* It may help explode those myths that fuel the pathetic Jewish Anglophilia. (280)

According to Sarah, then, anti-Semitism pervades English society, or certainly her own social milieu. In a sense, though, Zuckerman knows how to deal with the kind of up-front racism exhibited by Sarah; certainly he shows himself more than able to hold his own in their verbal exchanges. What really bothers him, as with the hero of *Deception*, is the more covert and insidious racism he finds in England. This subtler racism is discernible in Maria Freshfield herself, and this is where the more sinister aspects of the Rothian benign female are revealed. At one stage, for instance, Maria and Zuckerman are dining at a restaurant and a woman sitting nearby complains loudly that she needs a window opening because there is a terrible smell in the room. Zuckerman feels that this is directed at him

---

1   This is a description Zuckerman gives of Maria in Roth's autobiography, *The Facts*. Both characters make an appearance near the end of this book as Roth invites them to comment on the accuracy of his memoir. It is worth noting that Zuckerman is supposedly still living in England with Maria here and that he is sporting a beard which makes him look 'unmistakably Semitic' (*The Facts*, 185–6).

and he interprets it as a racist insult. '*Where* is the insult?' Maria asks him. 'She is hypersensitive to Jewish emanations' says Zuckerman. 'You're being absurd' Maria tells him' (219). Maybe Zuckerman *is* being absurd here (Roth leaves it for us to judge) but when he presses Maria about this issue her attitude is revealing. Though she ostensibly condemns racism and acknowledges that it does exist in English society, even in her own family, she seems less troubled by this than by Zuckerman's readiness to make an issue out of it. In other words, it is not racism but *conflict* that annoys Maria. Ethnic conflict, she suggests, 'makes life more difficult in a society where we're just trying to live amicably' (301). In short, anything that threatens the status quo is anathema to Zuckerman's English rose. To avoid conflict, however, she must ignore her own family's anti-Semitism, and essentially Maria's equanimity is revealed as compliance. She offers her own voice as the voice of reason whilst, at the same time, constructing dissent and difference as eccentric and negative. This is a condition, a way of thinking that Roth apparently sees as common in English society. He has Zuckerman say to her at one stage:

> the 'we-ness' here [in England] is starting to get me down. These people with their dream of the perfect, undiluted, unpolluted, unsmelly 'we'. Talk about Jewish tribalism—what is this insistence on homogeneity but a not very subtle form of *English* tribalism. What's so intolerable about to tolerating a few differences? (301)

Whereas in *Professor* Kepesh felt that England afforded him the freedom to throw off the shackles of his religious background, Zuckerman's Jewishness makes him feel uncomfortable, even threatened in English society. Inevitably this begins to affect the way he feels about his Jewish identity. In Israel Zuckerman had told Shuki that if he and Maria had a son he would not be particularly bothered about having him circumcised; he would not be concerned about asserting his Jewish identity because, presumably, the secular Zuckerman felt himself above these anachronistic and superstitious concerns. When he finds himself living in England, however, his opinion on this issue changes:

Only a few hours ago, I went so far as to tell Shuki Elchanan that
the custom of circumcision was probably irrelevant to my own
'I'. Well, it turns out to be easier to take that line on Dizengoff
Street than sitting here beside the Thames. (324)

In 'Christendom' Zuckerman is forced to take a position other than
that of enlightened, secular sceptic. In 'Christendom' Zuckerman
himself is in the midst of conflict in an environment where his
Jewish identity is threatened: as such he finds it impossible to be
blasé about his Jewishness. In other words, 'Christendom' becomes
an ironic comment on his Israel stories where Zuckerman was able
to present 'himself' as aloof and non-committal about Jewish issues.
In his fiction Zuckerman creates, firstly, a world in which he could
navigate a course between ideological differences (with his reason
and tolerance) and, secondly, one in which he must acknowledge his
own difference.

   Initially the notion Zuckerman has of England is hopelessly
romantic: England is a 'pastoral idyll.' Like Kepesh contemplating
life at the farmhouse at the close of *Professor*, Zuckerman comes to
England believing it to be a tranquil place where he can relax after
a life of conflict and controversy as a renegade Jewish writer. Thus
Zuckerman at first has a stereotypical and, perhaps one might say,
typically American idea of England that has its origins in books like
Washington Irving's *Sketch Book* (1819). Irving's England is one
'gleaming with refreshing verdure;' it 'abounds with every requisite,
either for studious retirement, tasteful gratification, or rural exercise' (Irving, 66–7). Zuckerman feels affection for just such an ideal
England and is bewitched by images of 'the mists and meadows of
Constable's England' and the promise of harmony and contentment
that he associates with it. What drew him to this, he tells us, is the
'idyllic scenario of redemption through the recovery of a sanitised,
confusionless life' (*Counterlife*, 322). This is what Zuckerman means
by the 'pastoral:' the 'perfectly safe, charmingly simple and satisfying
environment that is desire's homeland' (322). *The Counterlife* offers
a corrective to this view and, as Zuckerman is forced to revise his initial idea of England, so his Anglophilia is challenged. The allure of
the pastoral diminishes for Zuckerman when he comes to see that, as

he puts it, 'pastorals … cannot admit contradiction or conflict' (322). The pastoral cannot tolerate Zuckerman's difference and, although its methods of exclusion are subtle, they are nevertheless real. By the end of the book he realises that circumcision, something which for Maria is 'the very cornerstone of irrationality,' constitutes 'everything that the pastoral is not.' For Zuckerman circumcision comes to represent 'what the world is about, which isn't strife-less unity' (323). In other words, because conflict is inevitable, so the pastoral is unattainable, and those like Maria and her family who aspire to it are deluded, and dangerous. Just as Zuckerman's understanding of the Israeli conflict was flawed, then, so Zuckerman's notion of England is based on erroneous assumptions. Just as Zuckerman, the writer, created a distorted, fictional Israel, so Zuckerman the romantic American found himself drawn to a mythical England. 'Christendom' presents a shattered dream of tranquillity as the 'gentlest England has suddenly reared up and bit me on the neck' (307). Ironically, then, it is here he realises not only the inescapability of conflict but something of the appeal of conflict. It is desirable because it is healthy: Maria Freshfield's ideal of an England *without* conflict is a master-narrative of exclusion and denial—the England of urbanity and understatement is an England of complacency and culpable blindness. As suggested, an implicit parallel can be drawn between Maria's attitude in 'Christendom' and Zuckerman's in Israel. In Israel Zuckerman was able to offer his 'rational' view as a counter to Jewish extremism partly because he was an outsider, comfortably removed from the argument and its consequences. His refusal to commit himself either 'for' or 'against' stems partly from the fact that he does not have to. Maria can be dismissive of extremism and conflict too, not because she is an outsider, however, but because the so-called 'extremists' are outsiders. She is comfortably removed from the argument and is happy to keep it that way. Hers is the voice of an English upper class that is always going to label as extreme anything that threatens the status quo. Both Zuckerman in Israel and Maria in 'Christendom' feel that they are articulating the voice of reason but in England he realises that one person's reason is another's wilful blindness, that one person's rationality is another's racist complicity.

At the end of 'Christendom' Zuckerman comes to value his Jewishness. 'England's made a Jew of me in only eight weeks' (324), he tells us. What he comes to value most of all is his freedom to assert his Jewishness and to acknowledge the necessity of asserting it in a community which disapproves of difference. The custom of circumcision has marked Zuckerman as the 'counter' to someone else's 'other:' 'The heavy hand of human values falls upon you right at the start,' he says, 'marking your genitals as its own' (323). The inviolable reality of ethnic inheritance becomes a source of distinction and identity for Zuckerman. The novel ends with an image of an erect circumcised penis ('it's fitting to conclude with my erection' Zuckerman says, 'my circumcised erection' (324)): this is a symbol of difference which disrupts the English upper-class master-narrative of homogeneity.

In *The Counterlife* the desire to maintain social and cultural homogeneity represents a kind of dangerous absolutism reminiscent of Kepesh's experiences in Prague in *Professor*, and Zuckerman's in *The Prague Orgy*. It becomes symbolic of a totalizing, or totalitarian, way of thinking that stifles debate, denies difference and runs counter to all that Roth's literary postmodernism celebrates. *The Counterlife* quite literally rejoices in conflict, indicts homogeneity and implicitly values what might be termed a postmodern heterodoxy. The latter Zuckerman associates with America, a country in which, according to him, identity is always going to be less important because there 'people claim and disown 'identities' as easily as they slap on bumper stickers' (308). In England, by contrast, 'you are swathed permanently in what you are born with, encased for life in where you began' (308); and if England disapproves of where you began then it denies you the freedom to assert your identity. The ability to shift between identities is crucial for Roth's post-Kepesh heroes. We saw how Kepesh cannot function either as a professor or a rake, and even as a breast he must constantly change his life to find new ways of existing in extremis. Similarly, in *Zuckerman Bound* Zuckerman saw the necessity for adopting roles that correspond to the dissenting and conformist facets of his personality. An environment that limits his potential identities would clearly be anathema to such a hero;

given Zuckerman's 'irreconcilable halves' he must always—to cite the Rilke poem at the end of *The Breast*—have the latitude to 'change [his] life.'

As seen above, Roth himself has spoken out against the kind of English 'we-ness' that Zuckerman takes exception to in the novel. There is little doubt that the author's prolonged residency in England contributed to this attitude—for example, Hermione Lee, a friend of Roth's, refers to his 'increasing sense of cultural isolation in England' (11). In what he feels is the subtly xenophobic, homogenising atmosphere of England it seems Roth came to value difference: the difference inherent in his own Jewishness. If value resides in difference then the freedom to assert difference becomes all important: it necessitates a mode of articulation that can accommodate difference, and clearly this novel creates a space in which that can happen. *The Counterlife*, more than any previous Roth book, demonstrates the flexibility of the novel form. In the spirit of postmodernism, it refuses to be centred and—via its ontological trickiness—every position is under threat of contradiction. This novel asserts the impossibility and undesirability of the kind of 'strifeless unity' that Maria Freshfield desires, and, in its form and structure, it avoids offering a unifying narrative of its own. Against the absolutist ambitions of the English upper classes, then, Roth pits the dialogizing potential of the novel form itself. For Roth, as for writers like Salman Rushdie, the novel is 'a privileged arena'[1] that can encompass debate, contradict itself, undermine all assertions, even, as in this case, the ostensibly reasonable assertions of its own focalizing narrator. *The Counterlife* is indicative of the potential novels have to accommodate difference, counter-arguments and counter-lives.

Many English critics attacked Roth for his negative portrayal of English society in *The Counterlife*. The response he made to these attacks, in interview in 1993, is worth citing.

> If there is no anti-Semitism in Great Britain and if there is no group of people in Great Britain who hold anti-Semitic beliefs

---

1 The novel's 'privilege' according to Rushdie is that it is 'the arena of discourse, the place where the struggle of languages can be acted out.' See Salman Rushdie, 'Is Nothing Sacred' in *Imaginary Homelands*, 415–29.

> ... then I was mistaken in *The Counterlife*.... If, on the other hand, there *is* anti-Semitism in Great Britain, as perhaps there might be, and if there is a group of people in Great Britain who hold anti-Semitic beliefs, as perhaps there might be, then I wasn't mistaken ... and those scenes might not be the outpourings of a paranoid Jewish imagination as some of my English critics maintain, but in fact well within the range of English possibility.[1]

Just as in *The Counterlife* Roth juxtaposes assertion and counter-assertion here, demonstrating that, even in his interviews, he retains the scrupulously balanced, interrogative approach to argument that has characterised his post Kepesh books. Indeed, *The Counterlife* is the best example of this yet: it insists on allowing for and respecting counter-assertion, regardless of how irrational and even 'paranoid' it might at first appear.

So Kepesh's suspicions about the sustainability of the pastoral seen in *Professor* are recast here in a way that makes a point about the potentially malign nature of the pastoral mentality. Kepesh saw that *his* pastoral idyll was an unsustainable myth, and *The Counterlife* shows that it is also an unsettling myth, incompatible with what it means to be human. Where for Kepesh the pastoral life with Claire would mean a denial of his other self—the counter-self that drove him to Birgitta and Helen—for Zuckerman it implies a denial of ethnic difference, and the suppression of his potential counter-selves.

Counter-selves, Contradiction and Uncertainty

In *The Counterlife,* then, there is always a counter-story, an alternative version, even to the version that strives to sum up all versions. Likewise, there is always a counter-self: at one stage Zuckerman makes this point with reference to his own identity—there isn't an irreducible him that could be said to be the true him; rather he is akin to a troupe of players, different people in different contexts:

---

1   These are comments made by Roth in a BBC *Arena* documentary about his life and work. The programme was directed by Ronald Keating and broadcast on March 19th, 1993.

Being Zuckerman is one long performance and the very opposite of what is thought of as being oneself. In fact, those who most seem to be themselves appear to me people impersonating what they think they might like to be, believe they ought to be, or wish to be taken to be … if there even is a natural being, an irreducible self, it is rather small, I think, and may even be the root of all impersonation…. All I can tell you with certainty is that I, for one, have no self…. What I have instead are a variety of impersonations I can do, and not only of myself—a troupe of players that I have internalized, a permanent company of actors I can call on when a self is required. (*The Counterlife*, 319–21)

Clearly this is at odds with traditional notions of character as an integrated and irreducible thing. Once more we see Zuckerman exhibit Kepesh's sense of himself as a performer, and the latter's idea that the only way to become himself is to 'impersonate the self that I ought now to be' (*Professor*, 12). In *The Counterlife* there is no way of identifying the true Zuckerman, just as there is no way of determining the true story. The idea of the self as a troupe of players implies that each performance of self has potential legitimacy; and, the facts of the lived experience notwithstanding, the novelist is just as much of a performer. Just as there is no way of knowing the true Zuckerman, so there is no way of knowing the true Roth, and this notion of authorial ambiguity is one that Roth takes an increasing interest in as his career continues to develop. Indeed, the question of the relationship between Roth's biography and his art has been a topic of speculation for most of his writing life. Given the confessional feel of *Portnoy's Complaint*, many assumed this novel to be autobiographical, and despite obvious differences between Roth and his hero, similarities are numerous and obvious. Likewise, while the Kepesh books may not be autobiographical, the fact that the hero is a Jewish college lecturer interested in Kafka and Chekhov, and Roth has spent much of his career teaching in universities, mean the parallels can hardly be ignored. The Zuckerman books took this issue as a theme, and if anything augmented speculation about that relationship between the author and his character. He acknowledges the degree to which this is important in interview with *The Paris Review*:

> Think of the ventriloquist. He speaks so that his voice appears
> to proceed from someone at a distance from himself. But if he
> weren't in our line of vision you'd get no pleasure from his art at
> all. His art consists of being present and absent. (*Reading Myself*,
> 144)

Roth seems to feel that biographical speculation augments the appeal of his art. In the so-called 'Roth' books, Roth takes this a stage further by stressing the difficulty, even the futility, of making distinctions between fiction and biography. In these books he casts himself— or a character that bears his name and biographical details —as the protagonist, and we will now explore this theme in a little more detail.

In *Deception* Roth presents a series of dialogues where a novelist called Philip is apparently having an affair. In the middle of the dialogues Roth presents another set of dialogues in which the first set of dialogues is discovered by his wife. When she accuses him of having an affair he tells her that they were merely fictional notes for a novel. Then the adulterous dialogues resume, and we have no way of knowing if they are *indeed* fictional notes for a novel. This is further complicated by the fact that the dialogues relate things that actually happened in Roth's (i.e. the real Roth's) life and reference real life people, such as his brother Sandy. The original draft of the book also referenced his then partner Claire Bloom by name, but she forced him to use a fictional name by threatening legal action. She relates in her own autobiography, *Leaving a Doll's House* (1996), that her discovery of the dialogues and the accusation of adultery were things that actually happened. One of the interesting things about *Deception* is that it puts the reader in the same position as the apparently cuckolded wife: it's impossible to establish the truth-status of the narrative. Because there's no mediating narrator in *Deception* and it's presented solely as a series of scenes, the reader is denied a point of reference from which to make a judgement. This creates an environment of freedom for the protagonist that allows the conflicting aspects of his character to exist simultaneously. Once more, this environment of freedom creates a space for the synthesis of dissenter and conformist: in this case Philip the adulterer and Philip the husband exist simultaneously in an arena of ontological ambiguity.

In this respect it works very much the like those key symbols of unity in *The Breast, My Life as a Man, Professor,* and *Zuckerman Bound.* In *Deception* this symbolic space becomes crucial to the postmodern philosophy of uncertainty that was introduced in *The Breast*, not least because, as will be seen, it is linked to the issue of artistic freedom.

We can never know to what extent we are being deceived by *Deception*, then, and part of the book's point seems to be that this is always the case whenever we encounter language and narrative. Of all the dialogues that make up the novel, one of the most interesting is the conversation Philip has with an unnamed feminist critic. In this exchange, which takes place in an imaginary court of law, the critic accuses Philip of demeaning women in his work:

> 'Why do you publish books that cause women suffering? ...'
> 'Many people have read the work otherwise ...'
> 'Why do you depict women as shrews if not to malign them?'
> 'Why did Shakespeare?'
> 'You dare compare yourself to Shakespeare? ... Next you will be comparing yourself to Margaret Atwood and Alice Walker!'
> (Deception, 114)

The feminist critic is a stereotype, of course, presented as an ideologue with a bias toward particular ideas and texts. She goes on to ask him why, when he was working as a college professor, Philip felt justified in having sex with his students:

> 'How many times did you forcibly induce your students to fornicate with you?'
> 'There was no need to exert force'
> 'Only because of the power to influence and control implicit in the relationship.' (115)

Thus she accuses him of demeaning women through language (in his work as a writer) and of abusing his power over them (in his role as a college professor). Throughout the exchange she is shown to be hostile and bigoted, while Philip presents a calm and 'rational' argument; however, when it becomes clear that she will not be persuaded by his appeals to 'reason,' the episode takes a bizarre turn as Philip makes a pass at his detractor:

'Oh, you *are* a wonderful girl! You *are* clever! You *are* beautiful!'

'Your Honor, I must ask the court to instruct this *man* that I am not a 'girl'!'

'Come over here, prosecutor, would you please – '

'Your Honor, I *beg* you, the defendant is *blatantly* – '

'I want to ask your expert opinion about this – this – '

'Help, help, he's exploiting me, he's degrading me, he's attempting with this grotesque display of phallic – '

'You delicious, brilliant, lovely –'

'He's maligning me, Your Honour - in a court of law!'

'No, no, this is fucking, sweetheart—I'm fucking you in a court of law'. (117)

In a scene reminiscent of Portnoy's encounter with Naomi, it is implied that Philip advances on the woman and begins to molest her. As he does so he calls her 'wonderful,' 'clever,' and 'beautiful,' 'delicious,' 'brilliant' and 'lovely.' She responds, significantly, not by complaining that he is molesting her, but by crying 'He's maligning me, Your Honour.' He is frustrated because his appeals to 'reason' fail to register on the 'closed' mind of his antagonist, and the dialogue ends with Philip having abandoned rational debate. It is clear at the end of the exchange that Philip has become what his accuser suggests he is—an abuser of women. But first notice how the language he uses becomes perverted. Though Philip uses adjectives that are generally associated with praise ('wonderful,' 'clever,' 'beautiful,' 'delicious,' 'brilliant,' 'lovely') she claims that he is 'maligning' her. These words are interpreted as having opposite meanings to the ones they normally have. Just as the novel suggests that fact and fiction are often difficult to determine so, at a more fundamental level, the meaning of words is often ambiguous. Meaning is never fixed in other words. However, the feminist critic in *Deception* articulates a politically correct rhetoric which has ambitions to censor language and texts *based* on their meaning—hence her reluctance to accept that many read Philip's work differently to the women who are allegedly offended by it. Some of the other conversations Philip has are with people from behind the Iron Curtain and there is an implicit parallel drawn between the silence imposed by totalitarian regimes and the more insidious form of censorship Philip's feminist critic would enforce. They both proceed from the assumption that there is one right way of looking at the world, or the word: one ideology, one reading. It has been argued that Political Correctness has affinities with totalitarianism because, as Alain Piette suggests, 'it suffers no contradiction' (186). *Deception*, however, insists that, when it comes to language, everything is open to contradiction. Nothing is fixed because words and narrative always have the potential to deceive, to contradict. To attempt to censor words or novels based on their meaning can be seen as a totalitarian act, but it is also, in a sense, a pointless act because meaning can *never* be final or absolute. This is demonstrated eloquently in the scene cited above. Meaning depends not merely on the language employed, but also on context and interpretation. Thus, while the feminist critic accuses him of writing sexist and degrading novels, Philip insists that '[m]any people have read the work otherwise' (114). The implication is that novels, like words, are not in themselves sexist or degrading. Words are invariably polysemic; novels are always unfinished, dialogical and ambiguous. And just as we can't pin language down to a single meaning, it appears that we cannot pin Roth down either—we can't know where autobiography ends and fiction begins in this book, and so in this sense too it becomes a powerful expression of uncertainty, complicating any judgement we might want to make about the morality of authorship, or the hero's status as conformist or dissenter. So Roth's insistence on uncertainty is re-expressed here in relation to connections between fact and fiction, and linked to the issue of morality. This continues to be a theme in the 'Roth' books that follow, particularly so in the novel he published next, *Operation Shylock* (1993).

The Shrieking Contradiction: Operation Shylock and the Importance of Truth

We saw how the idea of contradiction is central to Kepesh's life and how it continues to be a key feature of Roth's thinking through the 80s and 90s. Where Kepesh was intent on resolving his contradictory halves, the Zuckerman books and *Deception* stress the inevitability and the importance of contradiction: life must always find ways of accommodating the counter-life. In order to explore how this notion relates to the issue of autobiographical truth, Roth begins to blur the ontological status of his heroes in quite elaborate ways, as seen in *The Counterlife* and *Deception*. He complicates the issue of truth and certainty to such a degree that Roth might at first sight appear to have given up on it, adopting the position of a relativist and relinquishing any sense of moral responsibility. However, in another of his 'Roth' books, *Operation Shylock*, Roth seems to stress the significance of truth, and reiterate the point made in *The Breast* about the importance of the search for meaning.

In *Operation Shylock* Roth learns that someone is touring Israel posing as him, Philip Roth, and advocating a philosophy called Diasporism which involves relocating Israeli Jews in Europe to save them from the potential consequences of an Arab-Israeli war. Roth visits Israel to confront this man, who turns out to be an ex-private detective from Chicago called Pipik. The relationship between Roth and his doppelganger is interesting and once again suggests a conformity/dissent opposition of the kind we have seen throughout Roth's fiction. Pipik—the other Roth—represents the dissenting facet of the protagonist's character: for one thing his philosophy of Diasporism is a threat to the Jewish homeland, advocating assimilation over tradition and threatening to 'undermine the integrity of Israel' (*Shylock*, 248–9). In other words, he becomes a threat to Jewish stability just as Roth himself was accused of being when he published *Portnoy's Complaint* (and Zuckerman when he published *Carnovsky*). Indeed, in many ways Pipik is the typical Rothian dissenter: he makes anti-Jewish diatribes whilst pretending to be someone else, just as Roth does via Portnoy, and Zuckerman does via Carnovsky: he is described variously as 'unshameable' (like Zuckerman the renegade writer), 'intemperate' (like Kepesh the rake), and 'driven by ungovernable compulsions' (like Portnoy) (368). As an agent of dissent Pipik represents disorder: he has the capacity to 'wreck people's orderly lives' (386). It is interesting to consider how the phenomenon of the doppelganger might relate to this. Claire Rosenfield, for instance, has written that doppelganger literature reveals a psychological conflict in the author between 'the constant menace of personal disintegration which apparently threatens us all and the loss of identity consequent…upon mental disorder' (344). It has been seen how the disruptive potential of dissent seems to haunt Roth, particularly perhaps in the Kepesh books where the hero fears the self-destruction threatened by the 'furnace' of unchecked desire. In *Operation Shylock* Pipik becomes nothing less than the personification of dissent, a representation of what the hero terms the 'usurping self beyond [his] control' (29). While Roth's doppelganger has all the traits of a dissenter, the protagonist—'Roth' himself—becomes a conformist. His double is deemed 'the lying Philip,' while he is 'the truth-telling Philip' (193), for instance, and 'Roth' comes to see his conflict with Pipik in terms of 'the responsible versus the reckless' (249). On one level, then, in the tradition of the doppelganger, both 'Roths' can be seen as aspects of the same character and the doppelganger theme provides the perfect opportunity for the author to construct a dialogue between conformist and dissenting selves. This theme is highlighted by the quote from Kierkegaard that prefaces the book: 'The whole content of my being shrieks in contradiction against myself' (9). It is significant that while the 'real,' conformist 'Roth' seems to get the upper hand in the novel, his dissenting other cannot be fully vanquished at the close, and he concludes: 'Pipik will follow me all the days of my life and I will dwell in the house of ambiguity forever' (307). This could so easily be Kepesh the scholar referring to *his* doppelganger, Kepesh the rake, and the 'menace of personal disintegration' which constantly threatens him.

In Israel 'Roth' is recruited as a Mossad agent by an Israeli spymaster, Smilesburger, in order to help track down individuals who have been giving money to the PLO. During the various interviews Roth gave whilst promoting the book he claimed that these events were *literally* true. It is very difficult to believe in them, however, not least because of the overtly comic way in which the story is presented. The names of the characters who are supposed to be real are often absurd: Smilesburger, Supposenick, Jinx Possesski, and Roth keeps drawing attention to the implausibility of the story, and its ridiculously convoluted plot. This reminds us again of Kepesh and his sense of the literary narratives that underpin his life (like Kafka and Chekhov), and again of Tarnopol who struggles to believe his so-called true story. Again it raises questions about the curious relationship between art and life. As in *Deception*, however, *Shylock* adds another dimension to this theme given that some of things Roth includes are plainly based on verifiable facts. For instance, while he is in Israel 'Roth' attends the trial of John Demjanchuk, the man accused of being Ivan the Terrible of Treblinka, something that the real Roth is known to have done. Demjanchuk maintains he is a victim of mistaken identity, and the problems associated with establishing the truth of his case parallel Roth's problem of establishing himself as the real Roth, not to mention the reader's problem of determining how much of this narrative *is* actually true. When making reference to Demjanchuk the phrase Roth uses is, 'There he was. Or wasn't.' The truth can't be established easily, and this extends to his own status in the novel, and indeed to the truth in general. In other words, Roth is once more making a point about the inevitability of uncertainty.

The story Roth tells in *Shylock* is outlandish, then, and every serious critic treated it as fiction for this reason. But this inevitably begs the question of whether this apparent outlandishness is a valid reason for assuming it isn't true? This is another interesting theme of the book and it is addressed with reference to the novelist Aaron Appelfeld whom Roth interviews whilst in Israel (this is also something that actually happened). Roth asks Appelfeld how it's possible to write about the Holocaust, and Appelfeld replies that it was 'far beyond the power of the imagination ... everything was so unbelievable that one seemed oneself to be fictional (56). In other words, just because the Holocaust seems too incredible to have happened doesn't mean that it didn't; by extension, as he states in 'Writing American Fiction,' given that reality always has the capacity to outstrip the imagination, in what sense is outlandishness grounds for calling the author of *Shylock* a liar?

While the truth may be difficult, perhaps impossible to establish, the reference to the trial of Demjanchuk underscores just how important it is to pursue it. In one sense the truth is always going to be elusive, but what are the consequences of giving up on it? It is a moral imperative to seek it. Where Philip in *Deception* seemed happy with ambiguity and the inevitability of contradiction, *Shylock* acknowledges the importance of the struggle to resolve doubt. While it may not be up to the artist to resolve conflict and establish certainty, the struggle is sometimes important and necessary. It was seen in *The Breast* how Roth seems to celebrate the struggle for truth despite the futility of the endeavour and *Shylock* once more underscores the validity of this desire.

While the theme of the doppelganger might reflect a split in the author's psyche and the threat of disintegration, it can also be seen as an expression of the hero's desire for unity. In the final chapter of his book *The Literature of the Second Self* (1972), C.F. Keppler argues that the construction of a doppelganger represents a desire for psychological integration and an attempt to unify the fragmented psyche on a symbolic level: it is an attempt to unite what Keppler feels is the split common to all men, the division between the individual and the collective. Keppler identifies 'a mutual hunger for the best of two mutually exclusive worlds ... of simultaneous differentiation and participation,' arguing that

> [t]he concept of ... an inclusive interconnection is difficult [and hence] writers of fiction have tended to express their sense of it by the specific case and the individual relationship, that of one to one, or one-half to one-half (actually it is always both). (209–10)

It has been seen how the self/society, dissent/conformity split is presented as a moral and psychological dilemma in Roth's work, and when viewed in these terms the doppelganger theme appears like another attempt to unify the conformity/dissent opposition on a symbolic level: another way of synthesising the familiar conflict; in Keppler's words it expresses 'the paradox of unity in duality' (210). Though Pipik is Roth's dissenting, disruptive other, then, there is a sense in which he needs the spirit of the other in order to be whole. Keppler writes how it is usually the case in stories of the second self that 'the intruder seems to have been invited to intrude, invited by the imagination that shaped him' (192); this certainly seems to be so in *Shylock* where 'Roth' actively seeks out his double, and though angered and frustrated by him, he is also stimulated: thus we're told that he conceives of Pipik as 'a great idea' (*Shylock*, 83), and while he might be annoying he is 'simultaneously electrifying' (70). The spirit of 'Pipikism' is summed-up by Smilesburger when he calls it 'the antitragic force that inconsequentializes everything—farcicalizes everything, trivializes everything, superficializes everything—our suffering Jews not excluded (389). It is the flipside of the Roth hero's seriousness and conformist sensibility: it is the 'antitragic' antithesis of seriousness. It is akin to the disruptive force that compels all of Roth's heroes: it is what lures Neil Klugman to the superficiality of Short Hills, what undermines Gabe Wallach's attempts to live a serious life, what informs Portnoy's antisocial bluster, what drives Kepesh's rakishness, and what makes a 'cutthroat caricaturist' and a pornographer out of Zuckerman. It is also, in equal opposition to conformity, what makes a writer out of the latter, and perhaps out of Roth too: to repeat what he says in *The Anatomy Lesson*: 'A novelist without his irreconcilable halves [is] someone who hasn't the means to make novels. Nor the right' (645). The 'farcicalizing' 'trivializing' spirit together with the conflicting compulsion to contain it is, it seems, what Roth's fiction is made of.

The Rake Triumphs: Sabbath's Theater

One of the few characters in Roth's fiction who is not overly debilitated by internal conflict is Mickey Sabbath, eponymous hero of *Sabbath's Theater* (1995). He is an elderly puppeteer who champions sexual transgression as a life-philosophy, but unlike Kepesh seems unperturbed by the consequences. Sabbath has no time for social mores, and is fiercely nonconformist. Like Kepesh he cannot tolerate commitment, but he fails to see this as a problem in his life and he seemingly lives with a clear conscience. The obligations and constraints born of religion, domesticity and nationhood are all anathema to Sabbath, but most of all he opposes prudishness and the so-called American Puritan ethic. His rejection of propriety and restraint is conveyed appropriately in the Otto Dix painting reproduced on the cover of early editions of the book: *Sailor and*

Girl (1925) shows an elderly sailor seducing a prostitute with a look of demonic intent in his eye. There is something simultaneously unsettling and engaging about this image of shameless sexual resolve that captures Sabbath perfectly. While we find Sabbath nauseating, there is arguably courage in his conviction that distinguishes him from the perpetually vacillating Kepesh: he is willing to surrender to his instincts without apology.

Sabbath finds an outlet for his libido and the perfect sexual partner in Drenka, his female alter-ego and comrade in sexual excess. Things change when Drenka is diagnosed with cancer and she asks Sabbath to commit to her in an orthodox relationship. For Sabbath this would constitute betrayal of his life-philosophy, capitulation to the narrative he despises. Drenka is a Croatian immigrant and Sabbath likens her demand for conformity to the tyranny of the Yugoslavian dictator she fled to America to escape: as he says to her at one stage, 'puritanism … is Titoism Drenka, inhuman Titoism, when it seeks to impose its norms on others by self-righteously repressing the satanic side of sex' (20). It will be recalled from *Professor* that Kepesh suggests a link between his impotence and the crushing weight of totalitarianism in Soviet ruled Czechoslovakia. The connection made between personal and social constraint can be seen as an effort to add another dimension to Kepesh's suffering: like the oppressed Czech people, Kepesh is diminished by his condition and the restrictions it places on his potential for expression; the connection is meant to give his personal frustrations a degree of gravitas. A similar connection with totalitarianism is made in *Deception* with Philip's potential censorship at the hands of feminism. Again with Sabbath, the parallel between domestic and political forms of oppression is supposed to add weight to the reader's sense of the hero's predicament and struggle: Sabbath sees his sexual non-conformity as a kind of anti-ideology, and to compromise his principles is no small thing. While he finally agrees to Drenka's demands, however, he rationalises it by describing monogamy as 'the final kick,' the only sexual role he has not experienced.

Of course the fact that either Sabbath or Drenka must yield to the other's values shows how easily demands for non-conformity can become just another controlling, repressive narrative. Their relationship, and their freedom, is sustained only if they share an ideology; as soon as this changes one becomes the oppressor and the other the oppressed. Sabbath in his role as determined anti-ideologue may sound like an advocate of freedom, but his own creed of resistance has an absolutist and oppressive potential of its own.

Sabbath struggles to preserve his freedoms, then, and the one freedom that he enjoys most of all is the freedom to shock and offend people. As we have seen in previous Roth novels, however, transgression always has potential consequences and human casualties: this is the case with Kepesh and all of Roth's dissenting heroes; from betrayed families to the broader Jewish community, people have been negatively affected by the Rothian hero's demand for unfettered self-expression. In *Sabbath* Roth takes his hero's willingness to offend about as far as it can go. Near the end of the novel, for instance, Sabbath is discovered by Drenka's son wrapped in the American flag, wearing a Jewish yarmulke, and urinating on Drenka's grave. Her son is understandably outraged:

> 'You desecrate my mother's grave. You desecrate the American flag. You desecrate your own people. With your stupid fucking prick out, wearing the skullcap of your own religion!'
> 'This is a religious act.'
> 'Wrapped in the flag!'
> 'Proudly, proudly.'
> 'Pissing!'
> 'My guts out.' (446)

Sabbath rejoices in insulting religion and nationhood, together with established codes of decency, but it's important to note how Sabbath's transgression can itself be seen as a 'religious act' of nihilism. This, like a religion, is what gives Sabbath's life meaning. Though he contemplates suicide after Drenka's death, the final lines of the novel make it clear that Sabbath's nihilism is his only reason for living: 'He could not fucking die. How could he leave? How could he go? Everything he hated was here' (451). Given that negativism and hate is Sabbath's *raison d'être* it is difficult to see the book as a celebration of the hero's individualism, as was the case with *Portnoy*; *Sabbath* is more complex and subtle than this.

Sabbath is a very engaging character and we can admire the courage of his relentless pursuit of individualism, while we also enjoy his verve and humour: as suggested, he is refreshing to the extent in which he is unlike Kepesh, but there is no sense in which the hero's dissent is endorsed here. At the end of *Sabbath's Theater* Roth makes it hard to see the worth of his hero's philosophy, fuelled as it is by hate. On one level Sabbath's nihilism seems to be the inevitable cost of the triumph of the rake, and of the refusal to compromise one's individualism. We saw how the struggle that animates Kepesh throughout *The Breast* and *Professor* is worthwhile, and the feeling was that we should admire his attempts to keep the rake in check: when dissent triumphs over conformity the consequences can be seen in a character like Sabbath. However, as always in Roth's post-Kepesh fiction, the book points in more than one direction. There is another way of looking at Sabbath, and that is as a man who is himself something of a contradiction. As David Brauner argues, all of Sabbath's negative traits have a positive dimension of sorts. While Sabbath claims to live outside narratives of morality, for instance, his intentionally immoral behaviour has a moral purpose, 'deliberately designed to expose the limitations of middle class liberalism, to excoriate bourgeois complacency (*Philip Roth*, 145). In this way he offers a corrective to hypocrisy, which is itself a moral act. Similarly, his 'forthrightness' might be considered courageous, and indeed edifying to those who, like Drenka, are receptive to Sabbath's liberating potential. Thus:

> His conduct—even, or perhaps especially, when most scandalous—is not arbitrary or anarchic, but rather part of what he calls 'the fight for the lost human cause,' a concerted campaign against the 'terrible lies' of those who misrepresent as 'sinister villainy' what is 'the ordinary grubbing about in reality of ordinary people.' (*Philip Roth*, 145)

Sabbath's insistence on embracing the rake can be viewed as a noble challenge to society's mendacious reluctance to accept normal human behaviour. Certainly the fact that it is possible to see a positive facet to Sabbath's unbridled dissent is suggestive again of Roth's interrogative approach to moral issues, and the balance that he introduced into his writing with Kepesh.

'It Makes No Sense:' Zuckerman Returns

Tolerating Shit: American Pastoral

As suggested, while Kepesh struggles with his contradictions, Roth's writer heroes are perhaps better able to appreciate that there is potential value in conflict, contradiction and doubt. We saw how Zuckerman comes to understand the importance of the writer's conflicting halves, and his performing selves; and when 'Roth' becomes his own protagonist he too finds his inescapable dissenting doppelganger 'electrifying' in *Operation Shylock*. In *American Pastoral* (1997), *I Married a Communist* (1998) and *The Human Stain* (2000) Roth continues to acknowledge the inevitability of conflict, chaos, and doubt; indeed, these books wage war against certainty and its various manifestations in utopian narratives such as the dream of an American pastoral, communism, puritanism, and political correctness. Together they constitute the American Trilogy, and again feature the writer-hero Nathan Zuckerman, though here his role is principally as storyteller, chronicling other people's lives against the backdrop of twentieth century American history.

We saw how the unviability of the pastoral became an issue at the end of *Professor*, and this was re-explored in terms of England and Englishness in *The Counterlife*. In *American Pastoral*, set mostly in the 1960s, the hero again aspires to an ideal: Swede Levov is an assimilated Jew whose ambition to live *his* version of the American Dream is undermined when his daughter becomes a terrorist; his pastoral idyll is challenged by unruly reality. Swede experiences 'the disruption of the anticipated American future that was simply to have unrolled out of the solid American past' (85); he discovers that life is not a simple, benign narrative unfurling into a predictable future: as with Kepesh in *The Breast*, catastrophe appears out of the blue, turning his world upside-down, initiating the Swede into another America entirely, the daughter and the decade blasting to smithereens his particular form of utopian thinking, the plague America infiltrating the Swede's castle and there infecting everyone. The daughter who transports him out of the longed-for American pastoral, into everything that is its antithesis and its enemy, into the fury, the violence, and the desperation of the counterpastoral—into the indigenous American berserk. (*Pastoral*, 86)

Initially the Swede thought he knew how the world worked, but by the end of his story he learns that—thanks to inevitability of chaos—uncertainty will always be a part of it, and everything is ultimately beyond his control.

Swede's daughter Merry, after becoming a terrorist, strives for a kind of purity of her own through Jainism: she takes its pursuit of non-violence to extremes, refusing to wash her body out of respect for the organisms that live on it. There's a section in the book where her father confronts her and, repulsed by her smell, flees the scene. It's suggested that if he'd responded to her differently he might have been able to save her and their relationship, but he does not have the stomach for it. The scene is representative of the Swede's attitude to life in general, suggesting that he can't, as it were, tolerate potentially disruptive 'shit'; he cannot abide his notion of wholesomeness to be tainted. It brings to mind Kristeva's interpretation of an individual's revulsion at the sight of corpses, and the 'unclean':

> [t]he corpse, seen without God and outside of science, is the utmost of abjection. It is death infecting life. Abject. It is something rejected from which one does not part, from which one does not protect oneself as from an object. Imaginary uncanniness and real threat, it beckons to us and ends up engulfing us. It is thus not lack of cleanliness or health that causes abjection but what disturbs identity, system, order. (Kristeva, 4)

We might see Swede's revulsion at the sight of shit as echoing Kepesh's fear of abjection, and his terror at the threat of a disruption to the order that underpins his life and constitutes his identity. Consider these words from David Brauner:

> With regard to Merry Levov, what Seymour fails to realise is that
> the smell of shit that clings to his daughter is not a sign of her
> decay but rather a sign of her impurity, of her failure to achieve a
> state of perfect purity (which can only mean death) and therefore
> of her continuing humanity. (*Philip Roth*, 164)

The implication is that 'shit' is an indication of our humanity, and
being tolerant of it, and able to reconcile oneself to it makes us more
human, more accommodating, and better able to live in a world that
is, after all, full of shit of one kind or another. As seen above, Sabbath
is one of Roth's heroes who *can* acknowledge this, and live with the
consequences. Swede can't because it is representative of everything
he is frightened of: the things that don't conform to his narrative of
rightness and purity. The implication of this novel is that sometimes
we need to be receptive to and tolerant of human nature, even at its
most unruly and embarrassing. To put it another way, as Kepesh notes
in *Professor*, we sometimes need to conquer our squeamishness—a
sentiment that seems to apply to everyone, and not just 'students of
literature.'

The book develops into a critique of the Swede's willingness to buy
into illusions, then, a tendency that the narrator, Nathan Zuckerman,
shared in his early years. Like almost everyone in the Jewish
community, the youthful Zuckerman is initially bewitched by Swede
Levov; at school Zuckerman was a classmate of the Swede's brother,
Jerry, and initially cannot comprehend why he is not as enamoured as
everyone else by the Swede's character and accomplishments: 'Since
I couldn't imagine anything better than being the Swede's brother—
short of being the Swede himself—I failed to understand that for
Jerry it might be difficult to imagine anything worse' (*Pastoral*, 6).
Interestingly, the Swede's supposedly positive traits—his good looks
and athleticism—are defined against Jerry's characteristics in a way
that creates an aesthetic and moral hierarchy. The latter is described
as 'a scrawny, small-headed, oddly overflexible boy' with a flair for
intellectual rather than physical pursuits (6); and, as Alex Hobbs
argues, the Swede's

> sign value (the social status afforded to his handsome appear-
> ance) is strengthened because it is juxtaposed against the image

of his brother…. Jerry is rendered almost sickly when compared to the Swede's robustness, and intellectual rather than physical. Despite its obvious advantages, intellectual capacity often carries negative implications in fiction; it is frequently associated with calculation or duplicity. Indeed, Jerry has the potential to outsmart others, but in relief to his sometime devious brother, the Swede stands as a simple and transparent moral force. (74–5)

As the novel begins to complicate the notion of the Swede as a 'moral force' (which it does, for instance, in his attitude to Merry), so Zuckerman's, and the community's, assumptions about how to read the world are exposed, and the importance of trying to interpret it with care and subtlety are underscored. *Pastoral* demonstrates how one's readiness to be seduced by the idyllic extends beyond the idealised environment, to the idealised individual; interpreting life in relation to any ideal implies a potentially pernicious misreading. It is to conceive of life as something that exists beyond history, and this is invariably a mistake: the ungovernable force of historical reality always has the possibility to make chaos, as the Swede, and Zuckerman begin to understand.

The conflict between order and chaos that troubles many of Roth's earlier protagonists, including Kepesh, can be seen again in this novel, then, and registers in its representation of Zuckerman's attitude to the Swede's relationship with his daughter. In a sense, where the Swede represents order, Merry represents chaos, and, as Aliki Varvogli has argued, Zuckerman is in a better position to relate to the latter than the former. Though he was initially enthralled by the Swede, Zuckerman eventually comes to see him as a completely unknowable character, totally unlike himself:

> By placing so much emphasis on his main character's unknow-ability and by repeating the fact that his protagonist is a man totally unlike him, Zuckerman implicitly admits the Swede's daughter, Merry, is far more knowable and comprehensible. Father and daughter represent conflicting American discourses. If he is Johnny Appleseed and represents an edenic vision of America, then his daughter is the serpent in the garden, and the novel suggests that, for an author writing at the end of the twen-

tieth century, it is hard to imagine, let alone sustain, a discourse
that imagines America as a prelapsarian Garden of Eden. (110)

While Zuckerman may feel that Merry is more 'knowable' than
the Swede, this obviously doesn't constitute an endorsement of her
actions; rather it suggests that she has an identifiable relationship
with her historical moment that the Swede doesn't seem to have; as a
result, Zuckerman can relate to and comprehend her actions in ways
that he cannot fathom the Swede. This has particular significance,
perhaps, given that Zuckerman is the storyteller in this novel,
implying that any meaningful representation of American reality
must fully acknowledge 'the serpent in the garden;' just as a writer
must, as Zuckerman says in *The Anatomy Lesson*, acknowledge his
own 'irreconcilable halves,' so he must address them in the world
exterior to himself. He must also acknowledge his fallibility, and
inability to access truth; as Nathan says in one of the most widely
quoted passages of the novel:

> The fact remains that getting people right is not what living is
> all about anyway. It's getting them wrong that is living, getting
> them wrong and wrong and wrong and then, on careful reconsid-
> eration, getting them wrong again. That's how we know we're
> alive: we're wrong. Maybe the best thing would be to forget
> being right or wrong about people and just go along for the ride.
> But if you can do that—well, lucky you. (*Pastoral*, 35)

Derek Parker Royal is right to suggest that 'there is something encouraging, even empowering, about this admission of
incomprehensibility;'[1] certainly it opens the mind to alternatives, and
keeps a check on reductive monologism and arrogant absolutism.
From a novelist's perspective, this need to admit uncertainty might be
said to necessitate an ironic perspective: a mode of telling that implicitly acknowledges the possibility of its opposite. Because Zuckerman
is the narrator of this story, his 'admission of incomprehensibility'
creates such an irony: with Zuckerman's narratives the reader is fully
aware that a counter-story is always a prospect, even an inevitability, and this awareness creates the kind of instability associated with

---

1   Derek Parker Royal 'Pastoral Dreams and National identity,' 195.

irony, underscoring the fact that narrative is never something that we can have faith in. The ironic perspective precludes certainty, and comes to be seen as a healthy one in Roth's work. Importantly the Swede is shown to lack irony; he thought he understood the world but is forced to revise this assumption: as Zuckerman says, he is compelled to learn 'the worst lesson that life can teach—that it makes no sense' (*Pastoral*, 81). This lesson comes too late, of course, and the novel links the Swede's credulousness with his inability to perceive irony; as Zuckerman says early in the book, 'there appeared to be not a drop of wit or irony to interfere with his golden gift for responsibility' (*Pastoral*, 5). Irony, or the capacity to entertain two alternatives simultaneously, is certainly crucial for a novelist, but the potential problems associated with its absence extend beyond the creative arts, a point that Roth will make again in the work that follows *American Pastoral*.

There's Only Error: I Married a Communist

The second instalment of the trilogy, *I Married a Communist,* is set in the 50s. It is about a man called Ira, the brother of Zuckerman's old teacher, Murray, who is persecuted for being a communist at the height of McCarthyism: in other words, Ira might be said to fall foul of a different narrative of purity, which in this instance is an ideology intolerant of radical politics. Like *Pastoral*, *Communist* becomes a critique of the possibility purity—and the denial of human nature—implicitly demanded by *any* utopian narrative. Ira himself aspires to a kind of purity in his own life—his youth having been blighted by juvenile delinquency and murder, he attempts to reinvent himself and achieve political and philosophical 'purity' via Communism. He marries a radio actress called Eve Frame who also needs to reinvent herself: she is embarrassed by her Jewish heritage to the point of anti-Semitism, raising an anti-Semitic daughter, and at one stage even referring to her own sister-in-law as a 'hideous, twisted little Jew' (253). In other words, they both try to rid themselves of those aspects of the self that they consider shameful; but both attempts at purification are seen as morally wanting. The point is that such utopian ambitions are not only untenable, but potentially dangerous.

This counts in both life and art. With regard to the latter, for instance, Nathan's old literature professor tells him that as a writer he must 'achieve mastery over [his own] idealism,' suggesting that idealising narratives inhibit creative thinking, precisely because they are at odds with our humanity: 'Nothing has a more sinister effect on art,' he tells Nathan, 'than an artist's desire to prove that he is good' (219); again we have a sense of the importance of contradictions for the artist. The costs of ignoring them are never good: we saw how when Kepesh endeavoured to repress his 'rakish' self he ended up turning into a breast; similarly, according to Murray, when writers try to do the equivalent this too has devastating consequences—they become bad writers. The book suggests that artists must always resit ideologies of any kind: narratives which generalise are antithetical to art. This point is made eloquently to Nathan by Leo Glucksman, an ex-G.I. studying for a literature Ph.D.: '"Politics is the great generalizer," Leo told me, "and literature is the great particulariser, and not only are they in inverse relationship to each other—they are in an antagonistic relationship"' (223). He argues that communism failed because its generalising spirit cannot accommodate chaos; the latter 'disturbs the organisation':

> Art also disturbs the organisation. Literature disturbs the organi-
> sation. Not because it is blatantly for or against, or even subtly for
> or against. It disturbs the organisation because it is not general.
> The intrinsic nature of the particular is to be particular, and the
> intrinsic nature of particularity is to fail to conform. Generalising
> suffering: there is Communism. Particularising suffering: there
> is literature. (223)

Bad art is like an ideology—it generalises and strives to make life conform; true art resides in the particular. Nathan—though not a bad writer—becomes a reclusive one later life (i.e. in the narrative present of *Communist*), cutting himself off from society and embracing a naïve narrative of purity himself. As far as Murray is concerned Nathan is in danger of romanticising the idea of the writer-recluse, or, as Brauner puts it, 'of subscribing to another version of the pastoral myth with which Ira deluded himself and eluded his history' (*Philip Roth*, 154). The potential for such delusion is inherent in the human condition and this, at the end of the novel, is the message that Zuckerman takes from Murray's story. Chaos, misunderstanding, and uncertainty typify our experience:

> 'It's all error, I said, 'Isn't that what you've been telling me?' There's only error. *There's* the heart of the world. Nobody finds his life. That *is* Life.' (319)

Certainty is an illusion, and error is an inevitable, inescapable fact of life. Such an insight is at odds with any ideology, but is wholly compatible with art.

The Ecstasy of Sanctimony: The Human Stain

The third, and arguably the most complex and interesting, book in the trilogy is *The Human Stain*. Set in the late 1990s, the utopian narratives under scrutiny here are American puritanism, and political correctness. Principally the novel is about how such narratives can never be compatible with the so-called human stain: or, to put it another way, with human nature. It is the story of Coleman Silk, a light-skinned African American who, like Eve Frame, and indeed like Portnoy and Zuckerman, doesn't want to be defined by his ethnic background. He begins to pass himself off as Jewish and becomes a classics professor at Athena College. During the course of his job he is accused of racism after inadvertently referring to two African American students as 'spooks.' Their cause is taken up by a staunch advocate of political correctness, Delphine Roux, and he is unfairly persecuted by the college authorities as a result of her zealous and uncompromising adherence to the dictates of political correctness; her unwillingness to admit the possibility that the word 'spooks' has been taken out of context. She is certain that she knows what kind of person Coleman is, and what motivates him. So the first irony of the novel is that this African American professor passing as a Jew is prosecuted for racism toward African Americans. A parallel to Roux's uncompromising version of political correctness can be seen in the way Bill Clinton was treated after the Monica Lewinski affair. The novel is critical of the hysterical response to Clinton's transgression that seemed to pervade American media and society in the late 90s.

Zuckerman calls it an 'ecstasy of sanctimony' and a 'piety binge' (2): oxymorons suggesting how people seem to actually enjoy this condemnation; and of course suggesting also that they are hypocritical. The novel argues that this has its roots in American puritanism; it's something that's never really gone away in American society since the early days of colonisation. Both PC and the Puritan narrative of moral rectitude are utopian narratives that fail to accommodate the human stain—they cannot tolerate fallibility or even differences of opinion. And the human stain is inevitable: it is what makes us human. The dangers of denial are as real for Coleman as they were for Kepesh: where repression has potentially turned Kepesh into a breast, denial makes Coleman less than human too: he tries to purify himself by denying the stain of his African American heritage, but to do so he must cut himself off from his own family, not least his mother. When Zuckerman learns Coleman's secret there is a sense in which the character seems to disappear for him: 'I couldn't imagine anything that could have made Coleman more of a mystery to me than this unmasking. Now I knew everything it was as though I knew nothing … he became not just an unknown but an uncohesive person' (333). It was seen how Zuckerman at the end of *The Counterlife* saw value in circumcision because it acknowledges difference and confers identity on the individual, and *Stain* reiterates that point. Coleman cuts himself off from his African American heritage because he refuses to be defined by it, but this loss of definition itself threatens his status as a cohesive person.

'The Worst Lesson that Life Can Teach': A Closer Look at The Human Stain

Like David Kepesh, Coleman Silk is a scholar hero, and in many ways *The Human Stain* has affinities with the campus novel genre. This is one aspect of the book that we will address in more detail here. As we have seen, Roth's American Trilogy as a whole suggests that the best education teaches what Milan Kundera calls 'the wisdom of uncertainty.'[1] The first two instalments, *American Pastoral* (1996)

---

1   Milan Kundera discusses his notion of the novel as a space where healthy scepticism can thrive in *The Art of the Novel*, 1988.

and *I Married and Communist* (1998), critique utopian narratives and in typical Roth fashion advocate doubt as a healthy alternative. In this respect they're indicative of Roth's postmodern fiction which, as argued earlier, invariably eschews a point of wisdom. However, while certainty seems an impossible and even dangerous ambition in these books, the desire for certainty is powerful. We saw how Kepesh struggles for the truth in *The Breast* regardless of the apparent futility of the project, and we saw again in *Shylock* how the importance of truth necessitates that struggle. This ambivalence is expressed eloquently by Zuckerman when he says of the Swede, hero of *American Pastoral*, 'he had learned the worst lesson that life can teach—that it makes no sense.' In Roth's fiction counter-arguments and counter-identities always threaten to undermine stability and coherence, but while the absence of a single truth or a single identity is painful, to desire it is inevitable. This section will discuss how this issue relates to *The Human Stain's* status as a campus novel, and particularly to the humour that some see as typical of that genre.

Commentators on the campus novel note that universities are often constructed as microcosms of society. Sally Dalton-Brown, for instance, cites David Lodge's point that 'inside, as outside, the 'academy,' the principal determinants of action are sex and the will to power (593). The same could be said of the fictional Athena College in Roth's novel. As suggested, the college's ex-Dean, Coleman Silk, is an African American who's spent his adult life passing as white; the power he craves is the power to shape his own destiny, free from the determinants of race. His overconfident belief in the validity of his decision to pass, and the general rightness of his point of view, bolster his illusion of a coherent identity. When he is accused of racism and refuses to apologise, his colleague, Delphine Roux, is instrumental in his dismissal. Like Coleman, she is arrogantly reluctant to tolerate contradiction, and like him she craves self-determination: she strives to be free of a family which, we are told, has no respect 'for the individual' (*Stain*, 275); and in keeping with Lodge's argument, power and desire motivate everything she does: she hates Coleman partly because she feels that he is a threat to her power, but is subconsciously drawn to him emotionally and sexually. Moreover, Delphine struggles to reconcile her status as a poststructuralist critic—a position she adopted to further her career—with strong emotional attachments to meaning and traditional thought, represented partly by Coleman and her repressed desire for him. Thus both Coleman and Delphine are conflicted characters who subconsciously crave integration, and both overcompensate for self-doubt with arrogant absolutism.

The world of Athena mirrors society in its tendency to embrace narratives of purity: as suggested, a parallel is drawn between Coleman's persecution for transgressing the campus codes of political correctness and the moralising Clinton encountered after his affair with Monica Lewinski. It's a symptom of America's unrealistic and hypocritical preoccupation with a Puritan ideal. Both Political Correctness and Puritan morality are seen as utopian narratives that fail to accommodate the human stain. People's tendency to exhibit blind faith in them is criticised, then, and a refrain that runs through the novel, and which is associated with Delphine's certainty that Coleman is culpable is, 'Everyone Knows.' Zuckerman picks up on this and the words he uses to criticise the fatuousness of such statements expresses one of the principal points of the novel:

> 'Nobody knows Professor Roux. What we know is that … nobody knows anything. You can't know anything. The things you know, you don't know…. Intention? Motive? Consequence? Meaning? All that we do not know is astonishing. Even more astonishing is what passes for knowing.' (209)

Once more certainty is unattainable and the pursuit of it is potentially pernicious. Indeed, Coleman and Delphine's misguided faith in their own positions is seen as a major character flaw. Interestingly their assumption that certainty is possible is related to a belief in a stable relationship between reality and language. We are told that Coleman inherited this from his father who taught him fastidiousness in language: 'My father … insisted on precision in my language, and I have kept faith with him. Words have meanings' (84). But Coleman is constantly misreading (at one stage finding meaning in a girlfriend's poem that 'didn't mean anything,' for example, and 'wasn't even a poem' (115)); and as the 'spooks' episode demonstrates, precision in language is an illusion. Delphine assumes that certainty is possible too, as her insistence that 'everyone knows' makes clear; and, like Coleman, she constantly misreads people and situations, including her own heart: as Zuckerman says of her: 'One's truth is known to no one and frequently—as in Delphine's very own case—to oneself least of all' (330).

Not surprisingly Coleman and Delphine's faith in certainty makes them both potentially bad teachers. Coleman is little short of reactionary is his response to Delphine's suggestion that there might be more than one way to teach the classics; while Delphine has taught herself to 'overcome the urge to capitulate' when her arguments don't work; she has learned to 'argue her point without backing down.' In both cases their misguided certainty is born of insecurity and a lack of coherent identity. In this sense both have similarities with recurring character types in modern campus fiction where, according to Robert F. Scott, the professors are plagued by '[s]elf-doubt, self-absorption, and self-hate' (83); Coleman and Delphine compensate for this with arrogant, misplaced conviction. They are like the typical campus characters that Sally Dalton-Brown identifies as comically foolish, framed in an 'environment that almost appears to encourage foolishness' (591). They belong to a long tradition of the scholar as comic fool that dates back to the *scholasticos* figure in the humour of classical antiquity: many of the jokes in the world's oldest jestbook, the *Philogelus*, for instance, feature a scholar fool whose lack of genuine wisdom is comically at odds with his professional status. Certainly both Coleman and Delphine are the butt of Roth's dark humour. Coleman's 'spooks' faux pas and its consequences are of course heavily ironic given that he is an African American; it marks a comic return of his repressed identity. The humour is compounded by Coleman's arrogance and his naïve conception of words as something he can have faith in. The joke Roth plays on Delphine, meanwhile, is equally ironic: she writes a lonely hearts advert soliciting a partner with identical traits to Coleman and hence revealing her subconscious desire for him. The joke is compounded by the fact that instead of emailing it to the *New York Review of Books*, she emails it to every member of her department at Athena. As with Coleman the joke has her reveal what she represses. In both cases the comedy is born of the character's wilful denial and psychological fragmentation, and their lack of insight is satirized. In both cases the jokes Roth plays on his scholar protagonists reveals a contrast between status and reality reminiscent of the comic scholasticos, and a humour that Dalton-Brown suggests remains central to the campus genre:

> The campus novel, as a satiric and comic genre, arguably belongs to that type of comedy called the comedy of degradation, which stresses the discovery of the base behind the lofty, of the paltry behind the great, of the ugly behind the beautiful, and of the absurd behind the obvious. (Dalton-Brown, 597)

Dalton-Brown cites Henri Bergson's theory of the comic as a way of reading this degradation, and it is worth considering this in relation to Roth's characters here. Bergson argues that comedy suggests a reduction of the living to the mechanical. In Bergson's scheme human beings are animated by *Élan vital*: a vital force driving both evolution and creativity. We have an innate awareness of this force, and an understanding of its essential nature, but whenever we lose sight of it we also lose sight of our humanness. In short, the comic is associated with those moments when we *do* lose sight of it, and laughter becomes our prompt to rediscover it again. When we lose touch with the 'living ideal' it creates incongruity which is revealed both through inappropriate physical behavior, and unsuitable language. Linguistic transgression constitutes what Bergson calls 'reciprocal interference,' an example being plays on words which break down the sense of harmony that 'exists between language and nature,' undermining the natural fluency of language (111). This is the case for Coleman and Delphine who, as suggested, are rendered comic within the world of Athena College by linguistic transgressions born of their psychological fragmentation. Coleman's 'spooks' faux pas contravenes campus society's demand for political correctness, rendering it out of step with the 'living ideal' in Bergson's terms; Delphine meanwhile is a poststructuralist (a specialist in the work of George Bataille) who is simultaneously drawn to Coleman's humanism, and those 'whose intention was to free the intelligence from the French sophistication' (266). In short she craves the certainty that poststructuralism precludes and is 'destabilised to the point of shame by [this] discrepancy' (*Stain*, 272) in her character. She struggles to reconcile who she is with who she feels she needs to be, and this creates conflicts that are manifest in her speech and which mark her as comically inept among her socially adroit colleagues. Thus her fellow scholars mock her way of speaking; 'they make fun of her language;' they 'ridicule' the vocabulary that 'she believes that to be a good literary critic she *has* to have.' (271) For both Coleman and Delphine, then, conflict and denial create linguistic slippages and idiosyncrasies that render them figures of fun in Bergson's terms. By contrast a character who appears to be in tune with Bergson's notion *Élan vital* is Coleman's young girlfriend, Faunia Farley. The classical connotations of Faunia's name, suggesting the rural deity of ancient mythology, adds to the considerable weight of such allusions in the book; but the name also has animalistic undertones, given the goat's horns, ears, legs, and tail that typify this god/dess. This contributes to our sense of her instinctiveness, her status as a child of nature, and, most importantly perhaps, of her dissimilarity to the cerebral Silk. Faunia works at Athena as a janitor, and we are told that she differs from the scholars in her freedom from 'the stupid glory of being right. From the ridiculous quest for significance' (171). Faunia is able to tolerate contradiction and uncertainty in ways that the academics are not. As a result, she refuses to let Coleman search for meaning in their sexual relationship: 'Don't fuck it up by thinking it's more than this… It doesn't have to be more than this' (228); she won't let him narrativise their lovemaking, and she refuses to tolerate teleological ambition, suggesting that questions like: 'is there a God?' and imperatives such as, 'What you're supposed to be, what you're supposed to do' 'just kills everything.' For Faunia, sex is 'the whole deal' (228–9). In the scene where she explains this to Coleman, Faunia, the supposedly illiterate younger woman, is effectively teaching the professor: Coleman asks her, 'Is that what this is—you teaching me?' and Faunia replies, 'it's about time somebody did. Yes, I'm teaching you' (229). This is an education that Coleman receives outside the academy, and in this sense the novel ostensibly privileges experience over scholarship; or at least experience over language. Faunia's celebration of instinctive sex suggests transcendence of the social and linguistic realm that has an almost spiritual dimension; indeed, at her funeral she is described as a pantheist. However, crucially, the novel stops short of romanticising

Faunia's position in this way—we are told, for instance, that the trait she shares with Coleman is an absence of something essential in her character; as Zuckerman says, 'she was quite lacking in something...a piece of her was decidedly not there' (212). In other words, the novel suggests that while there's no certainty or possibility of a stable identity within language, there's no possibility outside it either.

So *Stain* declines to endorse any position, and indeed goes out of its way to undermine its own authority, presenting its story self-consciously with constant intertextual allusions and metafictional self-reference that work to deconstruct its assertions. Like the pastoral scenes in *Professor*, *Stain* is overtly shown to be informed by pre-existing texts. For instance, the novel is presented in five chapters, referencing the five acts of a classical Greek play; the names of the characters—Faunia, Delphine, etc.—also allude to classical antiquity and the myths that underpin the oldest stories. Such allusions augment the patina of playfulness and irony in the book. In addition, it's impossible to forget that Coleman's story is presented by a professional storyteller, Nathan Zuckerman, and hence the product of a subjective imagination: another fallible human being renowned for making things up. His is just a version of events that must allow for counter-versions. Everything is under erasure in this novel, then, and Zuckerman's subjective reconstruction of events is merely a version among potential alternative versions. So the novel both critiques master narratives of certainty and refuses to become a master narrative itself. This playful, postmodernist tone is another facet of Roth's humour in the book, then, suggesting a reluctance to allow stability (in a manner that complements Delphine Roux's professed poststructuralism). *Stain* has this in common with other postmodern campus novels like, for instance, Gilbert Adair's *The Death of the Author* (1992), which according to Dalton-Brown, constructs 'an *aporia*, or impasse, a place of multiplicity of meaning forcing readers into the standard (post) modernist position of creating meaning out of the either/ors of the text' (598). Similarly, Roth's postmodernism apparently matches his message of doubt by denying the reader a single meaning.

Importantly, however, Roth's humour could also be said to work against his postmodernism. As we will now argue, while Roth's metafictional playfulness destabilises the text in one sense, another form of humour is present that seems to assert the possibility of certainty and coherent identity. Consider again the two key jokes that Roth plays on the protagonists. In the case of both Coleman and Delphine, the jokes reveal who they really are, integrating the duelling aspects of their character. Coleman's 'spooks' transgression marks the return of his repressed identity, and Delphine's personal ad reveals her humanist inclinations, and her sub-conscious desire for Coleman. In both cases the character's counter-selves find integration in the frame of the jokes made at their expense. As we saw, the joke Roth plays on Kepesh (his metamorphosis) does something similar, bringing together the warring facets of *his* character. Susan Purdie's Lacanian reading of humour may be of interest here. Like Bergson she sees incongruity as fundamental to humour, but she also explores its relationship to how we perceive the dislocation between the signifier and the signified. Discussing Purdie's reading of jokes, Gillian Pye says that when making a joke, the joker

> deliberately transgresses the one-to-one relationship of signifier to signified that generally governs signifying processes. He deliberately invokes more than one 'definitionally different' signifier or signified in one semantic space. In other words, he overloads signifying structures and in so doing draws attention to them. This marking of aberrant usage, the clear indication that the joker knows he is erring is…absolutely central to the nature of humour. In marking his error, the joker is effectively asserting his knowledge of the 'correct' procedures of signification, and thereby his identity as a fully competent 'master of discourse.' (56)

According to Purdie, jokers assert the possibility of integrated meaning by deliberately transgressing those structures that create the illusion that meaning is possible. The transgression is signalled as counter to the norm, and in this way jokers disrupt and simultaneously reinforce the illusion of coherence:

> [the joker] is motivated by the possibility of constructing control over discursive procedures that are actually unstable. When

the joker transgresses the rules by which unified meaning seems
possible, he is simultaneously touching on a fundamental exis-
tential anxiety. In other words, the comic attention is drawn to
the fact that subject identity itself is based on a sleight of hand;
on the illusory concept of plenitude. The latter is maintained by
the operation of the Symbolic, which acts as bridge between self
and other.... By touching on psychological incoherence and the
randomness of signifying structures, however, the joker is able
to mark such incoherence as aberrant, as abnormal. This balancing act, in which the possibility of unified meaning is reasserted,
may then be conflated with an (illusory) image of the coherence
of self. (57)

So jokers disrupt the rules of signification in order to suggest their
power over them, and to imply a stable relationship where there
isn't one, and in this way they bolster their image of a coherent self.
This is what happens in Roth's jokes here. The 'spooks' faux pas is
a joke about signification and the arbitrariness of meaning, implying
an aberration whilst simultaneously asserting 'the possibility of
unified meaning;' in other words, there is a desire for meaning
conveyed in Roth's narrative that parallels the subconscious desire
of his protagonist; it is an assertion of the coherence he requires
for a stable identity. The same goes for Delphine's email, 'an ad in
quest for a Coleman Silk duplicate or facsimile,' sent, as mentioned
earlier, 'not to the classified section of the *New York Review of Books*
but to every member of her department' (277). This joke is funny
because it constructs Delphine as a signifier who means two things
at once: what she purports to be and what she actually is are revealed
simultaneously within the frame of the joke, and the incongruity
between the two creates humour. In this instance Delphine herself
becomes a joke in which Roth 'overloads signifying structures and
in so doing draws attention to them' 'asserting his knowledge of the
"correct" procedures of signification,' and, again, 'the possibility of
unified meaning' and 'the image of the coherence of self.'

Purdie's Lacanian reading of joking suggests that 'humour
usually involves connecting inequitable relationships, whether they
are perceived in the world of the joke or in the world it represents,

with the fundamentally inequitable situation of subject identity itself' (Pye, 'Comedy' 60) and that is what happens in Roth's book. The two key comic moments in *The Human Stain* assert the fragmentation of reality and representation, but seek to reintegrate it. Within the frame of his novel Roth connects the 'inequitable relationship' of language and reality to the issue of Coleman and Delphine's irreconcilable counter-selves. In other words, this book seems to express a desire for unity akin to that which constantly informs Roth's post-Kepesh books. Throughout we have seen Roth's heroes struggle to accommodate the disruptive counter-self, and the jokes employed in this late novel work to serve that purpose: they are born of a need to unify antitheses, to integrate what the heroes are, on the one hand, and what they need to be on the other. But as with the symbolic expressions of unity in former works—Kafka's whore, Tarnopol's cross-dressing, Zuckerman's creations and performances, etc.—this expression of unity is unstable. The jokes construct a false impression of coherence, underscored by the fact that they occur within a postmodern context—i.e. within a novel that refuses to take itself seriously—which denies the possibility of meaning and coherence. As argued, the jokes suggest integration and fragmentation simultaneously, proclaiming the possibility of something that Roth's postmodernism suggests is impossible. The fact that Roth's jokes assert what his postmodernism denies teaches an appropriate lesson for a postmodern campus novel: it reinforces the Swede's painful insight about chaos and uncertainty: 'the worst lesson that life can teach—that it makes no sense.' We want it to, but it doesn't.

The Human Stain makes the point that, in a manner of speaking, everyone is a stain on someone's notion of purity—from Clinton on the Puritan narrative, to Coleman on Delphine's version of PC. What makes advocates of utopian narratives dangerous, of course, is their willingness—like Merry in *Pastoral* and Delphine in *Stain*— to blindly cling to them, intolerant of contradiction. In this sense *Stain* exposes the perilous potential of certainty and, even while lamenting the impossibility of certainty, warns us against the dangers of assuming it.

What is it that Puts Me Outside? *The Dying Animal*

The nature of the Edna O'Brian quotation that prefaces *The Dying Animal*, 'The body contains the life story as much as the brain,' suggests among other things that the latter should not be privileged over the former: the symbiosis is essential; thus Kepesh the cerebral scholar and Kepesh the instinctive rake are interdependent. The quotation seems appropriate for a book about the declining years of the character we know from *The Breast* and *Professor*. The title of the novella itself alludes to Yeats's poem 'Sailing to Byzantium':

> Consume my heart away; sick with desire
> And fastened to a dying animal
> It knows not what it is; and gather me
> Into the artifice of eternity. (204)

This is about aging, of course, and the things that the elderly body is forced to relinquish, most notably physical pleasure. If *The Breast* conveyed a desperate need to cling to life in whatever form, *The Dying Animal* acknowledges the fact that such a hold must eventually be relinquished.

Bridging the gaps in Kepesh's biography between *The Breast* and *The Dying Animal* is not an easy task; we assume—given his miraculous reappearance as a man in *The Dying Animal*—that his metamorphosis was either reversible, or a dream-state from which he emerged psychologically intact. Either way Kepesh fails to mention his time as a '155lb mammary gland' to the interlocutor to whom he narrates the final instalment of his story. It suggests perhaps that Roth is once more offering a postmodern challenge to coherence in fiction, reflecting the lack of coherence in life. Indeed, given that Kepesh's transformation into a breast was inexplicable, why should his transformation back into a man require explanation either? It suggests the extent to which individuals are at the mercy of forces beyond their control, perhaps, a theme that Roth has explored in previous novels and will return to again. But it isn't just the metamorphosis that doesn't feature; Kepesh's biography simply doesn't match up with the previous books, as one reviewer noted:

> Both the patient, sensible Claire and the histrionic Helen have been expunged from his memory in favour of an unnamed ex-wife who was an art restorer. This marriage couldn't have happened between the period covered by the previous Kepesh books and this one, since it produced a son who is 42. Simple arithmetic suggests that David, born in 1930 (two years before his creator), must have sired Kenny in his late 20's, during his marriage to Helen. Stranger still, Kepesh reminisces about taking Kenny on one of his annual retreats to his parents' Catskill hotel, which had, near the end of *The Professor of Desire*, been sold following the death of David's mother. (A. O. Scott, unpaginated)

The reviewer suggests that this could be a sign of Roth misremembering the provenance of his characters, but this seems unlikely. Much more likely is that Roth is making a point about the nature of storytelling. Readers of the Zuckerman and 'Roth' books will know how he loves to problematize the boundary between reality and fiction, disrupting expectations about the trajectory of characters. In *The Dying Animal* the anticipated 'plot' of Consuela's life is itself disrupted when she contracts cancer: Kepesh tells us that 'the loveliest fairy tale of childhood is that everything happens in order' (149), but Consuela's story shows that death can always undermine that narrative, and it is folly to have faith in it. Perhaps Roth's alternative history of Kepesh is meant to reinforce our sense of narrative instability, together with the notion of uncertainty and chaos that has become a theme in Roth's work.

We have seen how in former incarnations Kepesh struggled with commitment. Like most Roth heroes he is concerned with maintaining his autonomy to a point where it's difficult for him to fully engage with others on a human level. Typically, Roth's men are detached individuals who have been criticised for their tendency to objectify others, particularly women. At first sight this new version of Kepesh seems to belong to this tradition; indeed, as the trilogy has progressed Kepesh seems more comfortable about using his talents to manipulate people and to satisfy his desires; his struggles to stay in control of his own life are accompanied by an increasing willingness to control others. For example, his status as a TV and radio critic in *Animal* facilitates Kepesh's ability to seduce young, nubile students who, he nonchalantly admits, 'are helplessly drawn to celebrity, however inconsiderable mine may be' (*Animal*, 1). The guilty self-questioning that characterised the voice in *The Breast* has been replaced by a more self-assured narrative that might also make us feel that the professor is now more reconciled to the rake, and to the less sociable aspects of his character—so much so that he tells us that 'back in the mid-eighties the phone number of the sexual harassment hotline' was posted outside his office door (*Animal*, 5). Ostensibly, then, there seems to be much for which we might criticise Kepesh; however, several critics feel that Kepesh undergoes a significant transformation in this book, one that redeems both the character and his creator. Stephanie Cherolis, for instance, argues that

> At first glance, David Kepesh, in his most recent incarnation, appears to be a caricature of Roth's characters as described by his critics. He is crass and misogynistic toward women, shallow and devoted to the simple pleasures of life. The novel, however, crucially centres on a time of transition in Kepesh's life, a time when he must confront the loss of Consuela, a woman he truly came to love. Here, Kepesh's traditional coping methods, such as emotional distance as well as a rigid independence, are of no help to him, and he is left groping for reparation in the face of extraordinary pain. The novel tracks Kepesh's final stages in life from detachment to attachment, from the safety of solitude to the dangers of love and loss.' (14)

When Kepesh first sees Consuela he does indeed see her as on object: he is attracted principally to her breasts ('You see the cleavage immediately. And you see she knows it' (3)). Women appear to be there largely for his physical pleasure, and we are told how as a younger man Kepesh spurned commitment or emotional attachment to them. In this respect he is like his friend George who sees marriage as a cage; as Cherolis says, 'To these men, marriage, or attachment in general, disrupts the carefree sexual dynamic they hold dear by demanding something beyond the physical pleasure of sex. Attachment is a loss of control' (16). However, Kepesh's options as an older man are diminishing, as is his ability to attain this kind of sexual pleasure from women; this affects his ability to enjoy the degree of control he had over them in his youth. As he reflects on this power-shift he begins to think in terms of what he calls 'the pornography of jealousy,' which relates to his status as an aged man faced with the threat of losing his lover to someone younger. This concept is an interesting one that can best be described as a pornography of the imagination, creating suffering rather than pleasure:

> [t]he pornography of jealousy. The pornography of one's own destruction. I am rapt, I am enthralled, and yet I am enthralled *outside* the frame. What is it that puts me outside? It is age.... It's a representation, ordinary pornography. It's a fallen art form. It's not just make-believe, it's patently insincere.... Because you're an invisible accomplice in the act, ordinary pornography takes the torment out while mine keeps the torment in. In my pornography you identify yourself not with the satiate, with the person who is getting it, but with the person not getting it, with the person losing it, with the person who has lost. (*Animal* 41–2, emphasis in original)

In conventional pornography the male viewer achieves excitement by imagining themselves in the position of the male protagonist, but this is no longer an option for Kepesh; when he imagines his young lover coupling with a young man he can experience only the 'torment' and 'suffering' of jealousy. He is no longer able to objectify that experience of imagining sex because the suffering associated with the loss of potency and power takes precedence. In a sense, then, the 'pornography of jealousy' appeals to the emotions in a way that conventional pornography does not. The suffering accompanying 'the pornography of jealousy' engages Kepesh at an emotional level unachievable with regular pornography and, given the emotional distance he has always maintained, previously unachievable in Kepesh's life generally:

> Jealousy, an emotion evoked by the possibility of losing a possession, takes away the distance, and, in turn, the pleasure, from pornography. It does not offer the escapist fantasy of pornography; rather, it requires that pain become internalized and therefore an inextricable component of the sufferer's identity. (Cherolis, 18)

There is no longer the possibility of control and distance with 'the pornography of jealousy,' and likewise in Kepesh's relationship with women. His only option is to suffer. Suffering humanises him, however, and potentially enables him to engage in human affairs in previously unobtainable ways. Thus as an old man the formerly disengaged Kepesh is now able to experience the pain of the anticipated loss of Consuela, which is something we see at the end where he agonises over running to her bedside. And Roth develops this theme of emotional disengagement beyond the individual to society in general. The book suggests that society as whole is inclined to distance itself from reality. For instance, as Kepesh and Consuela watch the Millennial celebrations on TV, Kepesh is struck by what he sees as the 'triumph of the trivial' in the modern world, and the efforts people go to in order to detach themselves from experience. As Cherolis says, these celebrations lack significance for him, and he deems the extent to which people crave 'stimulation' as being a pathetic distraction from reality. Kepesh begins to see this phenomenon as nothing less than the behaviour of a world on the brink of destruction:

> No bombs go off, no blood is shed-the next bang you hear will be the boom of prosperity and the explosion of markets. The slightest lucidity about the misery made ordinary by our era sedated by the grandiose stimulation of the grandest illusion. Watching this hyped-up production of staged pandemonium, I have a sense of the moneyed world eagerly entering the prosperous dark ages. A night of human happiness to usher in barbarism.com. To welcome appropriately the shit and the kitsch of the new millennium. A night not to remember but to forget. (*Animal*, 145–6)

Kepesh seems to have come to the view that engagement with the reality of human life is important, not the distractions that block emotions. Consuela's suffering is something he cannot ignore, and in the face of it everything else seems trivial. Earlier in the novel George's diagnosis of Kepesh's suffering was that he had 'violated the law of aesthetic distance' (99) in his relationship with Consuela: he had fallen in love with her; but by the end of the story the implication seems to be that to maintain distance is to be in denial of reality, and not least of one's own capacity to love and to be human. In this sense the point is that Kepesh sees the value of relinquishing his position as detached critic and immersing himself in the human experience.

Thus it can be argued that Kepesh's relationship with Consuela is an edifying one, and the pupil teaches her former professor something important. This lesson begins in the moment Consuela rebels against Kepesh sexually. At one stage early in their relationship Kepesh is shown as being dissatisfied with Consuela's performance in bed, deeming her too detached, and he violently pushes his penis into her mouth in order to force her into the experience rather than have her remain 'passively supine' (30). After Kepesh has orgasmed an enraged Consuela bites hard at his member, snapping at it with her teeth. Though she doesn't actually bite it, this act adds an edge to the experience, not just for Consuela but for Kepesh too: 'Till then,' he tells us, 'it was all controlled narcissism' (31). Just as she needed to be 'freed from her own surveillance,' so does he, and it is after this episode that Kepesh becomes her subordinate in the relationship: 'It was the true beginning of her mastery—the mastery into which my mastery had initiated her. I am the author of her mastery of me' (32). Initially Kepesh teaches her the importance of engagement over distance in sex, and she ultimately teaches him the importance of emotional engagement in life. When Consuela returns to him as a dying woman he learns to appreciate her in new, and more human ways. For instance, when she asks Kepesh to photograph her body prior to her mastectomy, Kepesh no longer sees her as an object. As Aristie Trendel points out,

> In the picture-taking scene, the student's body is no longer an object as in the bite episode; its symbolic immortalization is under way, while at the same time Kepesh's transformation, radically different from the one he underwent in *The Breast*, is at stake. (56–65)

This all seems to suggest that Kepesh's world view changes, then: in teaching Kepesh how to suffer she humanises him, and enables him to see the shortcomings of emotional disengagement both for himself and for society. Given this shift in outlook we might assume that Kepesh will go to Consuela's side at the end of the story and demonstrate the degree of commitment that has previously been beyond him.

The idea that Consuela facilitates the possibility of human engagement for Kepesh is supported by Zoe Roth who reads the text in the light of George Bataille's theory of the relationship between death and desire. For Bataille, both represent the 'possibility of continuity,' breaking down barriers between individuals as discrete entities and destroying 'the self-contained character': erotic encounters always remind us of death, and 'always contain some kernel of this unsettling possibility,' reminding 'us constantly that death…stands there before us more real than life itself' (96). Ostensibly Kepesh views sex as something that reminds him that he is alive, of course, a kind of 'revenge' on death, and this pleasure gets more intense as he ages and the closer the proximity of death. But he can also be seen as being rather ambivalent toward sexual desire. For instance, it is significant that Kepesh always sees the object of his erotic desire in terms of art: according to Zoe Roth, Kepesh exhibits a 'sexual ethic that is rationally, almost coldly dependent on artistic representations—most commonly painting and music' (97). Viewing sex through the lens of art allows Kepesh to inoculate himself against 'the dangers of desire' (97). This is exactly what happens when he first encounters Consuela: he sees her as an art object with 'a polished forehead of a smooth Brancusi elegance,' and compares her to Velazquez's *The Maids of Honor*. Later he articulates his desire for her in terms of music, watching her mock-conducting and appreciating the spectacle of 'her breasts shifting beneath her blouse' (98). Later when he masturbates with Consuela in mind he plays Mozart's C Minor Sonata as an accompaniment. As Zoe Roth points out, for Bataille, art also has a relationship with death, 'offering us the vicarious spectacle of our own mortality' (98), and allowing us access to death without the reality of it:

Kepesh's careful codification of Consuela's body within certain generic registers is not only an appreciation of her form, but organizes a sacrificial scene that protects Kepesh from pain, loss, and death. Desire and art, as the prostheses of death, allow Kepesh to experience death vicariously, to separate himself from his own mortality while enjoying the erotic spectacle. (99)

When Consuela develops breast cancer, however, her status as an art object undergoes a significant shift for Kepesh. Importantly, he switches to another medium through which to view her: photography. The latter is different from art and music because it offers more possibility of unmediated representation: '[t]he paradox of the photographs he takes is that the supposed materialism of photography—its ability to capture reality unmediated and 'naked'—actually documents the beginning of the disease's decay of her body' (Zoe Roth, 99). Kepesh's first 'unmediated' exposure to the reality of Consuela, and the reality of death, affects a change in Kepesh. He is finally able to recognise Consuela's humanity: to see her as a human subject rather than an art object, and thus he is able to move 'beyond the strictly autonomous boundaries of his previous detachment' (100). Once exposed to Consuela as a mortal, imperfect entity he is no longer able to idealise or objectify her, and this again suggests a breakthrough in the way he relates to women and the world. It suggests that Kepesh might be able to do what he has never been able to manage before, to establish a meaningful connection with the world outside of himself. Again this points to the possibility of Kepesh committing himself to Consuela at the close of the story. However, it won't surprise readers familiar with Roth's interrogative method to learn that the novel can be seen differently.

Peter Mathews is one of several critics who argue that Kepesh's conformity-dissent contradictions once more remain unresolved in *Animal*. Matthews examines those scenes where Roth's hero looks back on the 1960s, the decade that created the liberal social circumstances that enabled his life of self-indulgence. According to Matthews, Kepesh's attitude to the 60s revolution is ambivalent partly because he viewed the counter-culture revolution as an outsider; he was able to *choose* whether or not to join in and this choice created an irresolvable dilemma for the Professor of Desire:

> Kepesh's problem lies in his contradictory desire to transform
> freedom, the revolution, something that by its very nature is fluid,
> dynamic, indefinable, and squeeze it into the suffocating rigid-
> ity of a philosophical system. The factor that repeatedly destroys
> the integrity—the health—of Kepesh's desire, therefore, is
> his 'pornographic' addiction to self-awareness. Outwardly, he
> preaches the Lawrentian value of instinct, of being spontaneous,
> of the beauty of unconscious grace, but his real pleasure in each
> instance lies in overturning these qualities both in himself and in
> the object of his lust. (51)

In other words, the difficulty of reconciling immersion with
disengagement is fundamental to Kepesh's character and, according
to Mathews, this persists until the end of the book; rather than seeing
the spectacle of the millennium celebrations as evidence of Kepesh's
new attitude, then, he sees it as confirmation that his view of the
world and his relationship to it hasn't changed at all:

> Consuela's discovery that she has cancer, coupled with the death
> of his close friend George O'Hearn, only reinforces Kepesh's
> role as a spectator: he is watching, bearing witness, not to the
> actual destruction of his personal world, but rather the narcissis-
> tic image he has created of it. It is this ambivalent hunger for the
> pornography of destruction that ruins not only the authenticity of
> Kepesh's approaching death but also reveals the underlying nihil-
> ism of his left-wing revolutionary politics. Kepesh's narcissism
> is destroying his instinctive vitality, the real 'dying animal' of the
> title: he does not want to be an animal, as Lawrence observes.
> He only wants to watch, via his intellect, the death throes of the
> existence he has imagined for himself. (53–4)

For Mathews, Kepesh ultimately spurns the emotional engagement
that might serve to humanise the old critic, and the real point of the
book is that he actually *retains* the perspective traditionally associated
with pornography: that of disengaged voyeur.

Given what we have seen of Roth's penchant for uncertainty, it is
hardly a surprise that the book should prompt antithetical readings.

Certainly Roth does not want to resolve the hero's dilemma in any obvious way, and this becomes clear at the end when Kepesh seems on the verge of making a commitment to his young lover. Up to this point the story has been told in the first person in what appears to be a monologue, but at the close we learn that Kepesh has been addressing a narratee who, as with Portnoy's Spielvogel, remains silent until the end. Kepesh tells his narratee that he has to go to Consuela's side: 'I have to go,' he says, 'She wants me there. She wants me to sleep in the bed with her there' (*Animal*, 156). Obviously going would be to demonstrate a degree of commitment at odds with Kepesh's ideals up to this point; it would mean compromising his life's philosophy, as his narratee points out when he tells Kepesh: 'If you go, you're finished' (156). We are left in no doubt about the significance of the dilemma; in a sense it is a life or death decision for Kepesh, as Debra Shostak points out:

> To go is to reject Kepesh's point of view, which has been devoted to the detachment necessary to self-gratification and even selfhood; to go is to accept his own death, with Consuela's—to be indeed finished. ('Roth and Gender,' 124)

According to Shostak, Kepesh's identity, his very character is at stake here, and to capitulate to emotion would constitute a metaphorical death. Certainly 'self-gratification,' has always been central to the hero's character, and to surrender to emotion would be inconsistent, and possibly even unconvincing from a psychological perspective.

As always in late Roth novels, uncertainty is maintained, and we never know if Kepesh goes to Consuela or not; of course, this has implications for how we relate to the novel. Frank Kermode in *The Sense of an Ending* writes of how we use the concept of beginnings and endings to make sense of our lives: we have 'a need in the moment of existence to belong, to be related to a beginning and to an end' (4); but Roth refuses to offer a satisfying beginning or ending to *The Dying Animal*. Just as we are denied an explanation for the hero's past and his former status as a breast, so we cannot be sure of his trajectory at the close of the story either. Just as Consuela's imminent death undermines the satisfying fairy-tale assumption that everything happens in order, so Roth denies us the comfort of familiar structures, or certainty.

At the end of the book Kepesh appears uncertain, and the reader must remain uncertain too. The familiar notion of stasis—i.e. the hero caught on the horns of a dilemma—is reinforced to some extent by Kepesh's treatment of Consuela as an art object. Throughout the book Kepesh appears like a critic struggling to make sense of Consuela: his inability to satisfactorily understand her and appreciate her relevance to his life mirrors his earlier struggles with Kafka and Chekhov. As in *The Breast* and *Professor*, art and life become confused again in *Animal*. Kepesh describes Consuela as having 'all the magical influence of a great work of art. Not the artist, but the work itself... she had only to be there, on view and the understanding of her importance flowed from me' (*Animal*, 37). Such reverent spectatorship inevitably renders Consuela inaccessible to him; his relationship with her is principally visual: she is perpetually 'on view' and he is a passive observer. He continually strives to interpret her, attempting to 'pin' meaning to her, either as 'student,' 'work of art,' or 'lover' but this struggle for interpretation simply foregrounds the inaccessibility of meaning: like all signifiers she is never a single thing, then, and there is a sense in which Kepesh's Consuela is lost along the chain of signifiers, deferred like Kepesh's insatiable desire. In his role as a critic he performs for her as a 'cultural authority. Her teacher' (32), suggesting that she can be taught how to fulfil his desires in the same way as she can be taught to deduce meaning from the art she studied under his tutelage. It is as if he strives to construct a version of Consuela as sexual protégé that suits his needs. But his signifier doesn't match the signified, and she quickly loses her sexual appeal. Thus Kepesh begins to describe her performances in the bedroom as perfunctory, 'a little like her mock conducting' (28). This epitomises the antithetical nature of Kepesh's struggle: his desperate search for cohesive meaning (and sexual fulfilment) is undermined by his inevitable inability to control and orchestrate his relationships, and to construct stable meanings; his loss of interest in Consuela sexually reminds us of his dissatisfaction with Claire in earlier books. Consuela like all signifiers is ambiguous and Kepesh's attempts to 'read' her are reminiscent of his quest to uncover the 'truth' of Chekhov and Kafka in *Professor*. It will be recalled that his visit to Prague in search of a deeper understanding of Kafka results in a complete impasse which delivers no reward either in terms of cultural enrichment or self-discovery; on the contrary, it leaves him all the more confused and dissatisfied, and mars what ought to have been a romantic holiday with Claire: his unease and dissatisfaction are manifest in his dream of Kafka's whore, a symbol that he struggles to interpret. Similarly, the true meaning of Consuela, his 'classic beauty,' frustratingly evades him and she becomes as intangible as his dream of Kafka's whore. So, just as the reader is denied the satisfaction of knowing the beginning and the end of Kepesh's story, Kepesh too is denied the comfort of certainty in his attempts to interpret his world, and the art object he constructs out of Consuela.

Misogyny, Commitment and Balance

Regardless of whether we see Kepesh as a misogynist, and regardless of whether he ultimately commits to Consuela, this book again offers an even-handed representation of the values it addresses. In one sense of course *Animal* presents a battle for power between the teacher and the student, and significantly this is a battle that Kepesh loses. In the early stages Kepesh has the upper hand, but as the novel progresses there is a power shift. As we have seen, this is initiated when Consuela 'bites back' at her teacher's penis, reminding him that she has human presence and a power of her own. He begins to fully recognise her humanity when she falls ill and they finally become equals as he is reminded that they share the common fate of all mortal beings. Interestingly, it is only when her humanity and materiality are revealed that she begins to find a voice in Kepesh's company, 'she began to speak about herself as she never had before, never had cause to before, as perhaps, she'd never even known herself before' (149). The implication is that this is the first time Kepesh really listens to her; formally she has only ever been an art object for Kepesh; either that or his student whose role is to be instructed. In this respect Kepesh is being criticised, and this is vital with regard to the way the book signifies. For the novel to be truly interrogative there must be a balanced approach to this conflict between teacher and pupil because it represents the classic Rothian dilemma, cast here as both a gender conflict and as a struggle between disengagement and commitment. Importantly, these elements of criticism create an undeniable spirit of balance. Kepesh's voice may dominate the narrative but his attitude and opinions are clearly interrogated and exposed. Indeed, Kepesh himself is aware of the fact that he doesn't 'universally compel admiration' as a man (*Animal*, 115), and of course this counts for readers too: we can see his shortcomings very clearly because they are made plain. Roth presents us with an image of masculine frailty in order to explore that frailty and how it might relate to contemporary gender politics, and he does it in a way that, crucially, does not privilege the masculine view; rather it exposes the masculine perspective, together with its prejudices and will to power.

With this in mind it is worth once more considering the issue of abjection. We saw Kepesh's abjection and dread of liminality and how it related to desire and terror in *The Breast*. Fear of the liminal was identified with the 'void'—the notion of copulating *as* a breast that would signify the ultimate debasement. Arguably in *Animal* Kepesh metaphorically falls into the void in two-fold fashion: by drinking Consuela's menstrual blood, and by forming the kind of emotional attachment with her that he has scrupulously avoided throughout his life. Ravaged by jealousy at the thought that age precludes him from satisfying Consuela indefinitely, he goes to the extremes of abjection by drinking her menstrual flow. Arguably a liminal substance in itself, the blood seals Kepesh's liminal status, signifying the death of his phallocentric power. In kneeling to Consuela in the bathroom, Kepesh becomes the suppliant victim of both her youth and her sexual power: neither of which he is able to master, his own body now in the process of degeneration. Here Kepesh believes that he is possessing Consuela when in fact it is the signification of his descent into the total abandonment of his masculinity. In his earlier incarnation as a breast Kepesh's masculinity was tried but not taken—his consciousness remaining inherently male—but here there is a sense in which submission to a woman during the essential process of femininity destroys it. It is not Kepesh who notes this descent but his friend, George, who unlike Kepesh upholds the 'law of aesthetic distance' with his women. According to George, Kepesh violated this law:

> The night she took the tampon out and you watched her bleed-ing—that was fine—but when you couldn't restrain yourself and went down on your knees.... Drinking her blood? That con-stituted the abandonment of an independent critical position, Dave.... You lick it. You consume it. You digest it. *She* pene-trates *you*. (*Animal*, 99)

Losing his masculinity in this way is the realisation of the fears pre-sented in *The Breast*: metamorphosis failed to conquer his masculin-ity, but Consuela, or more accurately his desperate need to possess her, succeeded in doing so, marking the metaphorical death of the one identity to which he has consistently clung: that of alpha-male.

Plots, Power and Unpredictable History

It is clear that *The Dying Animal* reinforces Roth's point about uncer-tainty and the inevitability of conflict. Just like the early Kepesh, not to mention most of Roth's heroes before and after, the older Kepesh shows what Zuckerman calls his 'irreconcilable halves.' Not only is he torn by the familiar psychological conflicts of desire versus restraint, and freedom versus commitment, but these conflicts extend to the world outside Kepesh. This notion is central to his status as a critic, and his philosophy of life, as he says at one stage:

> I am a critic, I am a teacher—didacticism is my destiny. Argument and counterargument is what history is made of. One either imposes one's ideas or one is imposed on. Like it or not, that's the predicament. There are always opposing forces, and so, unless one is inordinately fond of subordination, one is always at war. (*Animal*, 112)

Not only the individual, but reality itself is characterised by irrecon-cilable factions perpetually in conflict. For Kepesh history is a his-tory of struggle, and its course could always have been other than it was. Just as Kepesh can inexplicably turn into a breast, so his-tory can be unpredictable, and the apparently impossible or unthinkable is always a prospect. This is an idea that Roth explores in his 2004 novel, *The Plot Against America*. Here Roth invents a 1930/40s history of America in which the Hitler apologist Charles Lindbergh becomes president. He presents it as an autobiography, with himself and his family at the centre, and this has a markedly unsettling effect given the difficulty the reader sometimes has distinguishing between invention and historical reality. The consequences of having Lindbergh win the election are quite subtlety rendered: there are no concentration camps, or radical changes to the treatment of Jewish people, merely the threat that those changes are on the way. Just as it's difficult to untangle Roth's biography from fiction, so it's sometimes difficult to untangle fascist, racist America from the America of historical reality. This helps Roth generate a patina of authenticity in the book. He reinforces this by including a postscript to the novel, which, as Hana Wirth Nesher points out, is designed to 'persuade us of the plausibility, not only of the Lindbergh presidency, but also of the forces that would have been set in motion had this occurred' (170). Consider these words from Claudia Roth Pierpont:

> *The Plot Against America*, Roth concluded in the *Times*, had twin messages. First, that in spite of the general anti-Semitic discrimination by the Protestant hierarchy in the thirties, and despite the virulent Jew-hatred of the German American Bund, the Christian Front, Henry Ford, Father Coughlin, and, yes, Charles Lindbergh, it had not happened here—'How lucky we Americans are.' And second, that our lives as Americans are 'as precarious as anyone else's.' It might have happened like this. 'All the assurances are provisional,' he wrote, 'even here in a 200-year-old democracy.' The election of George W. Bush had affirmed, for him, the lesson not just of (*The Plot Against America*) but of all the books that he had been writing for years: 'We are ambushed, even as free Americans in a powerful republic armed to the teeth, by the unpredictability of history.' (278–9)

It was suggested earlier in this study that Roth and Kepesh sometimes sound alike, and that is the case here: they appear to offer very similar readings of the nature of history and society. For Roth the 'lesson of all the books that he had been writing for years' is exactly as Kepesh says in *Animal*, that 'there are always opposing forces,' both in the self and in society. History is the product of conflict, a power struggle between irreconcilable forces whose outcome can never be predicted. In this sense the idea of there being a plot in relation to history is ludicrous. As the stricken Consuela discovers in *Animal*, life doesn't have a predictable trajectory; and what's true of the individual life is true of life in general: as the Swede discovers in *Pastoral*, there are no predictable or manageable narratives.

We have seen how books such as *My Life as a Man*, *The Counterlife*, and *The Facts*, offer more than one account of a single story: in each case, no sole version of the story is seen to be 'true;' thus even the so-called 'My True Story' in *My Life as a Man* is inadequate without the subtleties and developments addressed in Tarnopol's 'Useful Fictions.' A point that Roth has made continuously is that a story is only ever a version. Roth develops this idea and applies it to American history in *The Plot Against America*. This is something he did before in *The Great American Novel,* which presents a comic rewriting of baseball history in the form of a monologue from a ranting old man called Smitty. This offered an alternative to what Roth has called the 'Official Version of Reality,' associated with the discourses of media and government. Smitty's account constructs an over-the-top conspiracy theory in a narrative full of explicit comedy: throughout the novel is peopled by caricatures and grotesques, and the tone is Rabelaisian and hyperbolic. Despite its extreme departure from realism, Roth spoke of his desire to suggest a link between fiction and the reality of American history in this novel; his stated aim was to 'establish a kind of passageway from the imaginary that comes to seem real to the real that comes to seem imaginary, a continuum between the credible incredible and the incredible credible' (*Reading Myself*, 91). As we saw earlier, the implications of 'Writing American Fiction' propose the emergence of an American reality that can outstrip the fiction writer's imagination; hence it's not impossible, perhaps, to conceive of American reality as being indistinguishable from the rantings of a madman, which is partly Roth's point. Roth re-examines this idea in *Plot*, but in a much subtler way. Where the over-the-top comedy of *The Great American Novel* makes it hard to give credence to Smitty's history, *Plot* renders the past with scrupulous realism; as Jason Siegel writes, Roth 'crafts his self-conscious fiction with exacting verisimilitude in order to argue by aesthetic means that the fiction he presents is as true as the factual history' (136). Siegel suggests that we are meant to see truth in Roth's alternative history, despite its departure from the facts. Just as in books like *The Counterlife*, where individual identity cannot be determined in relation to one single story of the self, so in *Plot* 'the national identity of the United States is not defined solely by the actual events that constitute its factual history, but also by its counterfactual history, which reveals undercurrents of fascism and anti-Semitism that were not activated in "real life"' (136). Just as Zuckerman in *The Counterlife* is defined by his life *and* his counter-life, so the truth of the past includes not just what happened, but also what *could* have happened: 'the multitudinous desires, contradictions, and potentialities' (Siegel,136), that help shape the past, also *constitute* the past; in this sense, what seems like a fictional version of history in *Plot* has the status of truth, as Siegel says:

> Roth's caustic satire strips the whitewash from American history to reveal its dark counter-histories...In this narration, history is converted from a static monologic text in which the White-Anglo-Saxon-Protestant-centered United States is depicted as0 the heroic nation that defeated Hitler to a dynamic dialogic work in progress whose counter-texts testify to the fascistic undercur-rents that perpetually threaten to disturb the surface of the dem-ocratic dream by victimizing ethnic minorities whose distinct experiences pluralize American history. (144)

This notion of history as a dialogue lends weight to the significance of the counter-narrative in Roth's work, and we are reminded again of the distinction that Roth made in 1985 between the 'written' and 'unwritten' worlds and what he sees as the perpetual, often confusing dialogue that takes place between the two.

We saw earlier that the familiar theme of individual freedom is once again central to *The Dying Animal*. The novel offers what one reviewer describes as a 'mediation on...the meaning of freedom' (Anon., 'The Savage Urge', unpaginated), and while we never know if Kepesh ultimately commits to Consuela or not, it is hard not to feel that freedom still means everything to him. Again this becomes a theme in *Plot*, as the hero, Philip, contemplates relinquishing the commitments and responsibilities associated with his Jewish identity: he wonders at one stage, for instance, if 'some Christian family will take me in and adopt me' (116); elsewhere he fantasises about being taken in by nuns 'as a familyless child' (222, 235), and about playing the role of a 'deaf mute' who would 'pretend not to hear, and nobody would find out who I was' (346). Throughout the book he has fantasies about breaking free from his family, and his Jewish heritage, and, as David Brauner suggests, these fantasies 'are not the romantic dreams of rebellion and self-liberation often entertained by older children ... but rather nightmares of self-annihilation; his flights of fancy become flights from the very idea of selfhood' (*Philip Roth*, 203). The young Philip fantasises about literally opting out of the world of conflict by stripping himself of the characteristics that define him: he reminds us of Coleman Silk, of course, but also a little of *The Breast*'s Kepesh who, in his metamorphosed state, enacts a retreat from the social world; most notably Philip's desire to relinquish language as a 'deaf mute' echoes Kepesh's Kafka-style yearning for a place free of words and the Symbolic Order; in other words a desire to jettison the social realm of inescapable division, conflict and contradiction. Certainly Philip, like Kepesh, feels he 'must change [his] life' in response to the shift in his circumstances; but once more the options are limited. While Philip has an impulse to abandon his roots, on the one hand, the importance of family is heavily stressed on the other. Inevitably the rise of fascism disrupts his family: his Aunt Evelyn becomes a Lindbergh supporter and is estranged as a consequence, for instance, and even Roth's brother Sandy is enamoured with Lindberg's vision; but ultimately family is a source of strength, safety, and order in the world. Discussing his father, Herman, Philip says,

> A displacement even greater than having to move to Union or to leave for Kentucky was to lose one's parents and be orphaned. Witness, [Herman] would tell you, what had happened to Alvin. Witness what had happened to his sister-in-law after Grandma had died. No one should be motherless and fatherless. Motherless

and father-less you are vulnerable to manipulation, to influences—you are rootless and you are vulnerable to everything. (358)

The absence of family would leave the individual defenceless and dislocated. This reminds us of how perilous Coleman Silk's decision was, of course, and it suggests too how meaningful family is generally for Roth's heroes, illustrating what is at stake when they rebel: as Timothy Parrish writes, 'reading Roth's oeuvre through *Plot*, one can understand what terrible personal risks were taken by Nathan Zuckerman or Philip Roth when they challenged their family order' ('Roth and Ethnic Identity,' 140). In *Plot*, the individualism so important to the likes of David Kepesh is equated with Lindbergh's isolationism; certainly this is how Herman sees the world: he interprets Lindbergh's America First politics as 'turning your back on your friends' and 'destroying everything America stands for' (84). So again there is a conflict between the individual and the collective expressed in this book, and again it is hard to see which is privileged. Emotionally the reader is likely to identify with Herman and his strong sense of loyalty to the family, but we cannot help but consider what the consequences of that are. In this instance Herman's demand for solidarity appears positive, but of course the moral implications of 'turning your back on your friends' is always dependent on who your friends are. In this novel, as in many others, the enemy again seems to be the notion of purity, whatever form that might take; and, as Ross Posnock, suggests, the ambiguity toward the self/community dilemma that can be seen at the close of *The Dying Animal*, registers again in *Plot*, offering a corrective to the young Philip's naïve certainty, and replacing it with a deeper understanding of the need to acknowledge and respond to contingency:

> That this possibility of change survives the bleakness of *The Dying Animal* testifies to Roth's gift for eluding any refuge of purism, be it sentimentality or despair, the better to nurture his respect for what in *The Plot Against America* bruises and strengthens his seven year old imagined self—the force of the 'unforeseen.' (32)

By the end of *Plot* Philip has come to see that he can't be sure of anything, and any response he might make to the demands of the self, or of his community, must always start from that premise.

The Late Novellas in the Light of Kepesh

How Much Longer Can There Be Girls? Everyman

Like all of Roth's later protagonists, Kepesh moves in a world of chaos: as suggested, there is no explanation for his change into a breast, or for his change back into a human being. There is no way of explaining or managing the conflicts and problems that disrupt his life, whether they come from within or without. Kepesh's internal conflicts are principally born of desire, but increasingly mortality comes to feature in his thinking, adding to his trauma. In the Kepesh stories the unpredictable and inexplicable nature of death is frequently stressed. It will be recalled that when Kepesh's father and Mr Barbatinik visit Kepesh and Claire at the end of *Professor*, Roth uses the idea of mortality to reinforce our sense of mutability and transience and qualify the seemingly idyllic closing scenes. Their appearance underscores the idea of inevitable change, and of the indiscriminate nature of suffering and death. Mr Barbatinik tells Kepesh and Claire of his ordeal in the Holocaust, an unfathomable nightmare of history survived more by luck than strategy, and of the death of his wife which likewise 'happened out of nowhere…How else?' (*Professor*, 258). The transforming nature of death is a theme in *Animal* too, of course, as the aging Kepesh begins to reflect on his own mortality; here too it is seen as capricious and indiscriminate in that it threatens Consuela in her early years, corrupting her youthful flesh. In this novel the desire for sex that has brought so much turbulence into Kepesh's life becomes a way of avenging death in life:

> To be chaste, to live without sex, well, how will you take the defeats, the compromises, the frustrations? By making more money, by making all the money you can? By making all the children you can? This helps but it's nothing like the other thing. Because the other thing is based in your physical being, in the

flesh that is born and the flesh that dies. Because only when you fuck is everything that you dislike in life and everything by which you are defeated in life momentarily revenged. Only then are you most cleanly alive and most cleanly yourself. It's not the sex that's the corruption—it's the rest. Sex isn't just friction and shallow fun. Sex is also revenge on death. Don't forget death. Don't ever forget it. Yes, sex too is limited in its power. I know very well how limited. But tell me, what power is greater? (*Animal*, 69)

The power of sex is why—in his metamorphosed state as a breast—Kepesh felt most detached from both himself and from society—he was impotent: neither 'cleanly alive' nor 'cleanly' himself. But while sex offers consolation of sorts, it does so at a price for a man like Kepesh who feels sex is the antithesis of order; he refers to it as the 'chaos of Eros,' suggesting that it is 'radical destabilisation that is its excitement' (20). This is why it has been impossible for Kepesh to live an ordered life of course; it is why, when he found he could derive pleasure from his nipple in *The Breast*, he was driven to near madness: 'I was afraid that if I became habituated to these practices, my appetites could only become progressively strange, until at last I reached a peak of disorientation from which I would fall—or leap-into the void' (see above). Even as a mammary gland—that most irrational of forms—he bows to rationality, forcing himself to 'tolerate the desire to insert my nipple into somebody's vagina' rather than succumb (*The Breast*, 2nd edition, 39). Clearly the idea of the disruptive chaos of desire and its effects on a man facing death interests Roth as it becomes a feature of his 2006 novel, *Everyman*.

The unnamed hero of this novel is a man in his seventies who sees death all around him: his friends are dying and he suffers himself with heart problems that keep returning him to hospital for surgery. There seems to be no logical reason why he should be plagued with ill health: he is the 'son of long-lived parents, the brother of a man six years his senior who was seemingly as fit has he'd been when he carried ball for Thomas Jefferson High;' but nevertheless, despite only being in his sixties, Everyman's 'body seemed threatened all the time,' and 'now eluding death seemed to have become the central business of his life and bodily decay his entire story' (71). As we know from *Animal*, ill health is indiscriminate, and we can sympathise with Everyman's sense of injustice. Following an operation to remove an obstruction in 'his left carotid artery' (67), however, he is philosophical: he understands that, in the face of indiscriminate suffering, 'there was nothing to be done. No fight to put up. You take it and endure it. Just give yourself over to it for as long as it lasts' (70). This is the resignation of a man who has come to view the world as Mr Barbatinik does in *Professor*: he recognises that suffering, 'happens out of nowhere.'

Like Kepesh's, Everyman's life has been disrupted by the 'chaos' of sexual desire. He experienced three marriages, and even the happiest of these was brought to an end by his inability to manage his desires. His second wife Phoebe ('the most helpful wife imaginable' (124)) is Everyman's equivalent to Kepesh's Claire, but despite her qualities he has an affair with a model half his age that destroys their life together. He sounds much like Kepesh when he says that the affair 'had been founded on boundless desire for a woman he had no business with but a desire that never lost its power to blind him and lead him, at fifty, to play a young man's game' (96). As with Kepesh, the 'chaos of Eros' was central to the appeal. Thus when he made love to this woman—who would later become his third wife, Merete—he would do so in his office at work regardless of, or more accurately because of, the risks: 'they couldn't stop what they were doing, where and how they were doing it, even though theirs was one of those office trapeze acts in which everyone has everything to lose' (109). There is a sense in which the affair happens almost against his will; like Kepesh Everyman values the ordered life, but there never seems a possibility of this being sustained: 'He hungered for something stable all the while he detested what he had. He was not a man who wished to live two lives. He held no grudge against the limitations or the comforts of conformity' (32). Despite his penchant for stability and conformity, after beginning his affair with Merete we're told that '[t]he young man who started out hoping never to live two lives was about to cleave himself open with a hatchet' (111). This brings to mind Kepesh en route to abjection, and his words interestingly echo

Kristeva's discussion of the deject, 'casting within himself the scalpel that carries out his separations' (Kristeva, 16). Clearly Everyman, like Kepesh, is torn from within. Unlike Kepesh, however, Everyman is not able to indulge his appetite for sex in later life. Kepesh in *Animal* knows that his sexual allure won't last forever, but he anticipates there being a possible consolation in art: Kepesh developed his skills as a pianist in response to his own question, 'How much longer can there possibly be girls?' (22). Similarly, Everyman hoped to find a creative outlet in retirement: he has a flair for art but as a younger man decided to forgo a career as an artist to take a job in advertising. While retirement offered an opportunity to fully explore the depths of his talent, however, he finds that he isn't the artist he thought he might be: the more he paints the more he is confronted with his status as a 'hopelessly laughable amateur' (128). Without this diversion he feels the absence of sex in his life even more acutely. At one point his desire is kindled by a young woman he meets while out jogging: though he engages her in conversation he is unable to take it further, and it is this thwarted desire that begins to define his experience of age; he describes this feeling as a sense of 'otherness:'

> A sense of otherness had overtaken him…. Nothing any longer kindled his curiosity or answered his needs, not his painting, not his family, not his neighbours, nothing except the young woman who jogged by him on the boardwalk in the morning. My God, he thought, the man I once was! The life that surrounded me! The force that was mine! No 'otherness' to be felt anywhere! Once upon a time I was a full human being (130).

Estranged from the majority of his family, without the consolation of a creative life, or particularly of sex with a woman he desires, Everyman's conflicts have led to loneliness. As a younger man he was also conflicted, but at least when he was conflicted he was, in a manner of speaking, complete: as with Kepesh, his desiring self and his conforming self combined to make a full—albeit indecisive— human being; however, with one of Everyman's halves missing, and the impossibility of embracing and being stimulated by the 'chaos of Eros,' he is half the person he was; as an old man he is something 'other' and alien to himself. Now his former self is just a memory that—as suggested by the phrase 'Once upon a time'—has little more substance than a fairy tale. This might make us want to reassess the Rothian dilemma and the trauma it creates for his heroes: at least when they were conflicted they knew that they were alive. Of course Everyman's status as a disengaged 'other' helps reinforce Roth's contention—reiterated repeatedly in his mature work—that conflict *is* life.

Just as the disruptive facet of Everyman's character surprised him, just as he found himself shocked by his own proclivity for disorder, so death comes unexpectedly. He enters hospital for what he assumes is routine surgery but dies on the operating table 'without even knowing it.' Everyman 'went under feeling far from felled, anything but doomed, eager yet again to be fulfilled, but nonetheless, he never woke up' (182). Once more what is stressed here is the degree to which the individual is subject to forces beyond his control, and while this reality can be energising and thrilling, and while we may flirt and titillate ourselves with chaos because it appeals to our ever-present desire to subvert order, we are forever at its mercy, so much so that reality can be alarming indeed.

'I Want to Be George Plimpton:' Exit Ghost

Everyman is an aging hero who cannot find compensation for old age in art: the pain of aging is augmented by the discovery that he lacks the aesthetic sensibility of someone like Kepesh. A Roth hero for whom the compensation of art *should* be available in later life, of course, is Nathan Zuckerman, and he re-emerges as an old man in *Exit Ghost* (2007).

After a long period of living as a recluse in the Berkshires he has decided to change his life once more and attempt to engage with the world. In his reclusive period Zuckerman has lived the equivalent of what for Kepesh would be the scholar's life: he has dedicated himself to his art, authoring the American Trilogy, which as we've seen charts America's history as reflected in the lives of Swede Levov, Ira Ringold, and Coleman Silk. A botched prostate operation has left him impotent and incontinent, and so Zuckerman cannot indulge the aspect of his character that informed his performance as a pornographer in *The Anatomy Lesson*. The quiet life has been forced on Zuckerman to some degree, then, and there is even a sense in which his impotence has enabled the production of the American Trilogy: prior to *American Pastoral*, Zuckerman had been wholly concerned with his own internal conflict but, as Matthew Shipe writes, '[h]is impotence paradoxically liberates him as a writer—allowing him to extend his artistic vision beyond himself—while it also shapes and to some extent limits, his imagination' (192). However, Zuckerman's friend, Larry Hollis, urges him to broaden his interests and seek a life beyond his writing, and when Larry dies Zuckerman decides to do just that. He travels to New York to undergo a medical procedure that might cure his incontinence. Answering an ad from a young couple interested in a house swap, he meets Jamie and Billy Logan, who are both writers. Jamie is beautiful and intelligent and Zuckerman instantly becomes infatuated with her. Unlike with Kepesh and Consuela there is no chance that this incongruous match can be consummated, of course, but that doesn't stop him desiring her: she has, he tells us, 'a huge gravitational pull on the ghost of my desire' (66) and he indulges it even though that 'desire made her the biggest problem in my life' (177). When he first meets them at their apartment Strauss's *Four Last Songs* is on the CD player, and we are clearly meant to see this as a comment on the aging artist: Zuckerman wonders if his arrival had prompted the couple 'to play such dramatically elegiac, ravishingly emotional music written by a very old man at the end of his life' (34). Zuckerman's desire for Jamie inspires him to write a play, *He and She*, taking the form of a stripped down dialogue between a man and a woman, rather like the dialogues in *Deception*. In his stage directions for the piece Zuckerman indicates that *Four Last Songs* should be playing at the beginning of the drama; this is appropriate, he tells us, because it is a piece in which '[t]he composer drops all masks and, at the age of eighty-two, stands before you naked' (124). The implication is that this is what Zuckerman is doing in *He and She*; as Matthew Shipe suggests,

> Within Zuckerman's appreciation of Strauss, we can view the
> impetus behind his final work of fiction. No longer interested in

> (or capable of) sustaining the elaborate fiction that he produced
> during the American Trilogy, Zuckerman strips the artifice away
> from his fiction and reduces it to its core: a male and female
> voice talking. (197)

Like the composer of *Last Songs* Zuckerman has reworked his aesthetic to suit his capabilities: no longer concealed by artifice, he
exposes himself in his most elemental form. The story is a reworking
of Zuckerman's 'real life' encounter with Jamie in which he explores
the consequences of his desire for her. It is, according to Zuckerman,
a 'play of desire and temptation and flirtation and agony'—the very
things that inform Kepesh's life too, of course, and that are fundamental to the Rothian dilemma. For Roth's heroes, agony is generally
an accompaniment to desire, certainly this is so for Kepesh in all his
incarnations, but a writer hero like Zuckerman can make use of such
agony in ways the critic cannot. Indeed, where would Zuckerman's
art be *without* agony? There is a sense in which Zuckerman the writer
seeks out agony, and this is really what prompted him to change his
life and return to the city. He wonders if the enterprise should be
titled, '*A Man in Diapers*. A book about knowing where to go for
your agony and then going there for it' (41).

   In his adoration of the young and beautiful Jamie, Zuckerman. like
Kepesh in *Animal*, experiences the 'pornography of jealousy.' The
aging, impotent Zuckerman cannot make love to this woman but he
can imagine her making love to a younger man. The latter comes
in the form of a twenty-eight-year old writer, Richard Kliman; he
is a friend of the Logans and wants Zuckerman's help in compil-
ing a book about his old hero E.I. Lonoff. The attractive, intelligent,
over-confident Kliman reminds Zuckerman of himself as a younger
man, and Zuckerman torments himself with the notion of Kliman
being Jamie's lover. After a heated exchange between Kliman and
Zuckerman, Jamie defends Kliman, throwing Zuckerman into a state
of anguished envy: 'I preferred not to think too graphically about
why she was arguing the case of the serious man who had been a
boyfriend at college and with whom (I could imagine all too easily)
the link had remained sexual even after her marriage to devoted
Billy' (108). The pornography of jealousy makes Zuckerman suffer

as Kepesh did, but unlike Kepesh, Zuckerman the writer is able to utilise his agony. He makes it the subject of *He and She*, dramatizing his suffering in a context that redeems it. At one point Zuckerman explains why the artist needs to torture himself in this way, why he needs to dramatize, and in the process identifies the compensation that can be found in art:

> But isn't one's pain quotient shocking enough without fictional amplification, without giving things an intensity that is ephemeral in life and sometimes even unseen? Not for some. For some very, very few that amplification evolving uncertainly out of nothing, constitutes their only assurance, and the unlived, the surmise, fully drawn in print on paper, is the life whose meaning comes to matter most. (147)

In Zuckerman's *He and She* that 'amplification' sees his fictional surrogate, He, explore the pornography of jealousy still further. When he asks Jamie's fictional incarnation, She, about her past relationships, he tells her that it is because 'I want to die of jealousy' (231). The tragedy of the hero's position in the play—his pain and frustration at never being able to fully have what he craves—is what gives the story its power and meaning, and by extension it is what gives power and meaning to Zuckerman himself: it is through his writing and his fictional incarnation that he can be 'fully drawn' and give significance to his pain. In art, then, Zuckerman is able to achieve a degree of 'assurance' and perhaps a degree of substance and satisfaction that Everyman lacked.

The novel closes with Zuckerman back in the Berkshires where he produces the final scene of *He and She*: in 'reality' Jamie turned down his offer of a relationship, while in the play She accepts. She agrees to meet him in his hotel room; however, given that He knows what the only conclusion of such a meeting could be, her acceptance terrifies rather than satisfies the hero and He 'gets out as fast as he can' (292). We are told that his fictional surrogate 'disintegrates,' and the implication is that this will be Zuckerman's last fiction. The writer is suffering from increasing memory loss and his mind is letting him down. The aging, incontinent Zuckerman frames a fiction in which his hero is animated, not by his desires, but like him by the ghost of his desires, and in the closing lines his disintegration suggests that his failure to satiate them is paralleled by his failure to exist.

Throughout his career Zuckerman has struggled to reconcile life and art: the former has fuelled the latter and this has caused him problems. As a young writer his work threw him into conflict with his father, and the Jewish Community; indeed, we learn in *Exit Ghost* that one of the reasons behind his retreat into the Berkshires was the receipt of anti-Semitic hate mail. His dilemma has been like Kepesh's in that he has struggled to live life on his own terms: to reconcile the conflicting impulses that make him what he is. Throughout his work we have seen that Roth constructs images and metaphors that offer transient fantasies of integration for his conflicted protagonists, or which symbolically solve the dilemma that torments them, and in *Exist Ghost* this comes in the form of Zuckerman's reference to a real person, George Plimpton. When Zuckerman learns that he has died he begins to reflect on the life of this man who, like him, drew on his life for his art. Plimpton would write books about sport constructing himself—or a bumbling version of himself—as an inadequate amateur: 'In *Out of My League* the easy-going master of self-possession goes so far as to envy the poise of the Yankee batboy; in *Paper Lion* he pretends he hardly knew how to hold a football' (249). In doing this he didn't make himself look a fool; on the contrary, 'he succeeded in maximising his glamour rather than repudiating it' (249). As a result, everyone loved and admired Plimpton, and he manages to achieve the perfect balance between art and life that Zuckerman craves. As he says at one stage, 'When people say to themselves 'I want to be happy,' they could as well be saying 'I want to be George Plimpton': one achieves, one is productive, and there is pleasure and ease in all of it' (250). Thus from Zuckerman's tormented perspective, Plimpton has managed to reconcile art and life in a way that he has not: Plimpton's art is born of fun rather than agony, and in producing it he has consolidated rather than compromised his place in society.

Be Greater than Your Feelings: Indignation

Age is less of an issue in Roth's 2009 novel, *Indignation*, although the theme of death is again central. Here focus moves back to the 1950s: it will be recalled that this decade provides such a crippling atmosphere of constraint for heroes like Gabe Wallach and Tarnopol earlier in Roth's career, and dictates the shape and tone of his early writing. This time the protagonist, Marcus Messner, is another ostensibly good Jewish boy: like Kepesh he is a devoted son who feels stifled by his home life. Indeed, he feels parental interference as acutely as Portnoy, although in Messner's case the culprit is his overbearing father: 'I left because suddenly my father had no faith even in my ability to cross the street by myself. I left because my father's surveillance had become insufferable' (2009). Like Kepesh, Messner had a happy childhood and as a younger man 'had a great talent for being satisfied' (15), but he increasingly finds that in order to achieve happiness he must, again like Kepesh, change his life. In the first instance this means seeking a university as far away as possible from his father: he chooses Ohio's Winesburg College, a fifteen-hour drive from his home city of Newark; not only is it geographically remote, but as a conservative Christian college it also constitutes a cultural departure for this son of a kosher butcher. In many respects the college resembles Bucknell University, which Roth himself attended in the 50s, and many of the college traditions Messner encounters featured in Roth's own life as an undergraduate. One such tradition is the obligatory attendance at church services, something that rankles with the atheistic Messner; as he says to Winesburg's Dean:

> I object to having to attend chapel forty times before I graduate in order to earn a degree.... I do not need the sermons of professional moralists to tell me how I should act. I certainly don't need any God to tell me how. (100)

As with Kepesh, then, the devoted son has a rebellious dimension. There were signs of this as a child, and just as Kepesh was drawn to the ribald, rebellious comedy of Herbie Bratasky, so the young Messner warms to the humour of Big Mendelson who worked in his father's butcher's shop. 'I was seven or eight, and because he has this nasty kind of humour and because they called him Big Mendelson, I thought he was the funniest man on earth. Finally my father had to get rid of him' (137). Messner makes sure that his father won't always be around to 'get rid of' potential bad influences when he moves to Winesburg, of course, but even out of his father's reach he encounters restrictions that seem to thwart his efforts to live life on his own terms. For one thing, the campus mores encroaching on Messner's freedom extend beyond compulsory chapel attendance to include sexual conduct. As with Kepesh, Messner is drawn against his better judgement to an unsuitable woman who comes in the form of Olivia, a beautiful fellow student with a history of mental illness and self-harm. In one sense she is Messner's Helen: a captivating force who appeals to his id, but who threatens to ruin his life; she is the exact opposite of the woman his parents would want for him:

> I had fallen in love with—or I had fallen in love with the folly of falling in love with—the very girl my father must have been imagining me in bed with on that first night he'd locked me out of the house. (75)

It seems to be transgression itself that motivates Messner, who has 'fallen in love with the folly of falling in love.' Messner himself cannot fathom it, just as he cannot fathom his equally powerful will to conform, illustrated beautifully when he finds himself in the Dean's office:

> I had not expected to hear myself saying 'sir' to the dean, though it was not unusual for timidity—taking the form of great humility—to all but overwhelm me whenever I first had to confront a person of authority…. 'I don't mind calling you sir, Dean.' I did, though. I hated it. That's why I was doing it! I wanted to take the word 'sir' and stick it up his ass for singling me out to come to his office to be grilled like this. I was a straight A student. Why wasn't that good enough for everybody? I worked on weekends. Why wasn't that good enough for everybody? I couldn't even get my first blowjob without wondering while I was getting it what had gone wrong to allow me to get it. Why wasn't *that* good

enough for everybody? What more was I supposed to do to prove my worth to people? (84)

Messner had attempted to change his life, moving away from home in an effort to establish a degree of autonomy, but he encounters more constraints on his freedom. Like Portnoy he is dismayed that the advocates of duty and conformity won't leave him alone, and despite his best efforts he cannot seem to appease them. Also like Portnoy, and of course like Kepesh too, the impulse to submit is set squarely against the desire to rebel. Messner is torn by the familiar conflict, then, and this bewilders and frightens him: despite his serious attempts to work hard at college, he finds himself at odds with the system and its rules. The conflict jeopardises his place at Winesburg, but worse still it endangers his life given that to save himself from the draft he must retain his status as a student. Early in the novel we find that he has been unsuccessful in doing so—significantly, he tells us this after relating the incident where he unexpectedly receives fellatio from Olivia on their first date:

> What happened next I had to puzzle over for weeks afterward. And even dead, as I am and have been for I don't know how long, I try to reconstruct the mores that reigned over campus and to recapitulate the troubled efforts to elude those mores that fostered the series of mishaps ending in my death at the age of nineteen. (54)

Messner is like Kepesh of *The Breast* in that he is reflecting on his life—and his transgressions—from a place of isolation. He assumes he is dead, although we eventually learn that he is under morphine, having been injured in the war he was desperate to avoid. He is trying to make sense of a predicament which is as unfathomable as Kepesh's metamorphosis, but which seems to have been born of a similar conflict, a similar inability to control his dissenting impulses, which in Messner's case drew him inevitably to Olivia. We are told that when Messner's mother met Olivia and saw her character and her problems, she begged her son to abandon her:

> You be greater than your feelings. I don't demand this of you— life does. Otherwise you'll be washed away by feelings. You'll

be washed out to sea and never seen again. Feelings can be life's biggest problem. Feelings can play the most terrible tricks. (175)

Though he promises not to see Olivia, ultimately Messner is not 'greater than his feelings.' When Olivia suddenly disappears from college he cannot prevent himself from obsessing about her, and this leads him back into confrontation with the Dean. This conflict deepens when the Dean learns that Messner has been hiring someone to attend chapel on his behalf, and Messner refuses to apologise for this. Messner's dissenting impulses eventually cause his downfall, and we learn that after expulsion from college he was drafted into the army only to be wounded in Korea: for the duration of his narrative Messner has been in a morphine-induced coma. In the chapter 'Out from Under' Messner's coma comes to an end, his consciousness fades and he dies. It is left to an anonymous third person narrator to reflect on the hero's life, making the point that he has been killed essentially by his defiance and indignation; it was his inability to avoid saying 'fuck you' to those seeking to supress his individualism that killed him: 'Yes, the good old defiant American 'Fuck you,' and that was it for the butcher's son, dead three months short of his twentieth birthday' (231). But as with Kepesh's metamorphosis in *The Breast*, and Consuela's cancer in *Animal*, it is the inexplicability and apparent meaningless of the situation that is stressed. Certainly Messner cannot make sense of it; his father can't make sense of it either, but he seems closest to a point of wisdom in this book: we are told that his son dies before he had chance to learn 'what his uneducated father has been trying so hard to teach him all along: of the terrible, the incomprehensible way one's most banal, incidental, even comical choices achieve the most disproportionate result' (231). Life and its eventual conclusion are 'incomprehensible,' sometimes comically so; certainly there is a degree of mordant comedy in the fact that we eventually discover the pointlessness of Messner's rebellion: in the book's final 'Historical Note' we learn that in 1971 'to the horror of no authorities other than those by then retired from administering Winesburg's affairs—the chapel requirement was abolished along with virtually all the strictures and parietal rules regulating student conduct' (233). In other words, Messner raged against traditions that were eventually abolished without anyone really caring, a point which adds a Kafkan sense of futility to Messner's life. But it is hard to see Messner as a victim of his socio-historical moment: the impression we get is that, even without 1950s college restrictions, Messner would have found some other need to rebel, and some other reason to be guilty about it. As suggested above, it is transgression itself that motivates him; he cannot help saying 'fuck you.' Hence there is a feeling of inevitability about the hero's trauma that is typical of Roth heroes, and which again is typical of Kafka. We have the sense in Kafka that his heroes could elect to walk away from their problems rather than engage with them, if they had the strength or perhaps even the desire to do so. This is the case with Josef K., in *The Trial*, for instance, who is representative of many Kafkan heroes in the extent to which he seems to be tried by the court of his own conscience. This is often true of Roth's heroes too, particularly for characters like Portnoy whose suffering is comically irrational, for Zuckerman who seeks conflict to fuel his art, and Kepesh, who is tormented by conflicts that most men can manage without turning into a breast.

The Omnipotence of Caprice: The Humbling

We have seen how important the idea of performance is to Roth's heroes: Kepesh conceives of his alternative ways of being as 'roles,' for instance, and role-playing is central to Zuckerman's writing, and his sense of self throughout the books in which he features. *The Humbling*—Roth's penultimate novel—is partly about what happens when an individual loses his ability to perform. This is the fate of Simon Axler, a sixty-five-year old actor who suddenly finds himself unable to act. Just as there is no reason for Kepesh's transformation into a breast, so Axler 'lost his magic as an actor for no good reason' (16). The experience makes him suicidal and he commits himself to a psychiatric hospital, but finds that his depression lifts, not as a result of the therapy he receives, but, again, for no clear reason. Once more Roth makes a point about the individual being at the mercy of chaos: "'Nothing has a good reason for happening," he said to the doctor later that day. "You lose, you gain—it's all caprice. The omnipotence of caprice. The likelihood of reversal. Yes, the unpredictable reversal and its power"' (17). Here again we see the inevitability of the unpredictable in Roth's work and how individuals are subject to brute chance and contingency. Just as Kepesh says in *Animal*, 'there are always opposing forces,' so Axler acknowledges 'the unpredictable reversal and its power'.

Unable to practice his art, unable to perform, Axler finds himself largely incapable of social engagement; like Zuckerman of the American Trilogy, he cuts himself off from the world until meeting up with Pegeen Stapleford, the daughter of two old actor friends. She is twenty-five years his junior and experiencing a transformation of her own: though formerly a lesbian, she becomes Axler's lover and the two embark on an affair that offers him a degree of fulfilment where everything else has failed. Importantly, Axler is almost wholly passive in this relationship: while he assists Pegeen financially in her transformation into a more 'feminine' looking woman, it is she who directs the changes. He pays for her clothes and expensive haircut, and ostensibly she appears to 'submit to his ministrations,' but the power lies squarely with her, as the narrator makes clear: it was she 'who had taken him over completely, taken him up and taken him over' (66). The power to act/change is crucial in this book, and where Axler no longer has ability to perform/transform, Pegeen does have alternative roles at her disposal; she can still recreate herself, as seen in the rediscovery of her heterosexuality and the adoption of a more conventionally feminine appearance. The power to create roles for oneself equates to power itself in the story, and, again, while Axler is powerless, Pegeen is not. This can be seen in their sexual life where Pegeen is the one who takes control; at the outset of their lovemaking, for instance, we are told that 'he lay on his back and she mounted him' (91), and even when Axler initiates contact with a woman for a *ménage à trois* he recognises that Pegeen is the dominant party: 'He thought, I am providing her Tracy the way I give her clothes…It dawned on him that he was ceding all the power to Pegeen' (110). There is a sense in which the loss of Axler's creative spark has unmanned him, then, and he feels the force of this when Tracy joins their lovemaking. Where Axler is no longer convincingly potent, Pegeen is. When the lovemaking begins Axler 'would not participate until summoned' (112), and it is Pegeen who is sexually animated and forceful. The ability to create a role for oneself seems key to being sexually active rather than passive. This is very different from Kepesh's encounter with Elisabeth and Birgitta in Europe where the male hero is the centre of the proceedings. By contrast, in Axler's case we are told that, as a virtual non-participant in the sex, 'it looked as if he was the one who would end up crying in the corner of the room' (112). Now that he can no longer perform he feels his limitations in sexual situations just as he does in social situations: he is an observer in the lovemaking, just as he is an observer in life. Consider this scene where Axler watches Pegeen's performance with Tracey:

> There was something primitive about it now, this woman-on-woman violence, as though, in the room filled with shadows, Pegeen were a magical composite of shaman, acrobat, and animal. It was as if she were wearing a mask on her genitals, a weird totem mask, that made her into what she was not and was not supposed to be. (113)

Pegeen retains the ability to make herself 'into what she was not' and the novel implies that this degree of performance/creativity is crucial to sex and to life. When eventually he *does* contribute to the lovemaking scene, his sexual performance, like his acting, lacks conviction. Pegeen directs Axler to 'Defile her' and his response is unconvincing, 'Three children got together,' he says, 'and decided to put on a play, whereupon his performance began' (114). Needless to say that this 'performance' is a flop, and when it is over, it's Pegeen rather than Axler who Tracy kissed 'passionately,' and the encounter is a catalyst for the breakdown of his relationship with Pegeen.

Before Pegeen finally leaves Axler he begins to fantasise about a possible future with her that would involve them having a child together. He seeks the advice of a doctor and becomes elated at the prospect: 'Axler felt ecstatic with the return of his force and his naturalness and the abandonment of his humiliation and the end of his disappearance from the world' (121). At this point we have the impression that Axler is, for want of a better phrase, groping for a way of being alive, which is something that Kepesh and all of Roth's protagonists have done. As someone who has lost his ability to create roles for himself, or adopt alternative roles at will, however, there are limited ways forward for him; as a result, it is as if he must revert to what he feels is his core masculine identity and the 'naturalness' associated with man's most basic function as procreator. He harbours this fantasy of fulfilment until Pegeen tells him she is leaving and he realises it's no longer a possibility. At this point he sees no way forward, no way of living meaningfully in the world: 'He could no more figure out how to play the elderly lover abandoned by the mistress twenty-five years his junior than he's been able to figure out how to play Macbeth' (133). When Axler can no longer perform, he is limited to being himself, or rather to ways of life that don't require masks or invented identities: this is what he hoped to achieve through fatherhood, but when this is denied him he lacks the imaginative resources to reinvent himself; unlike Kepesh or previous Roth heroes, he cannot even attempt to change his life; he cannot even conceive of alternatives, let alone embrace them or execute them convincingly. All he can do is kill himself. However, even suicide doesn't come easily for someone who has lost the ability to perform: the implication is that this too is a role, as Axler himself says to his fellow patients at the psychiatric hospital:

> 'Suicide is the role you write for yourself,' he told them. 'You inhabit it and you enact it. All carefully staged—where will they find you and how will they find you.' Then he added, 'But one performance only.' (15)

But Axler—devoid of his creative spark—struggles to write this role for himself; rather, like Kepesh in *Professor*, he must search for a pre-existing narrative that will make sense of his predicament and, in this case, facilitate a way out of it. He imagines himself in a story by Chekhov:

> Finally it occurred to him to imagine he was committing suicide in a play. In a play by Chekhov. What could be more fitting? It would constitute his return to acting, and, preposterous, disgraced,

> feeble little being that he was, a lesbian's thirteen month mistake,
> it would take everything in him to get the job done. To succeed
> one last time to make the imagined real he would have to pretend
> that the attic was a theatre and that he was Konstantin Gavrilovich
> Treplev in the concluding scene of *The Seagull*. (140)

For Axler the ability to practice his art was his only way of living in
the world, and it is the only way of dying in it too. Earlier we saw how
for Philip Rahv Rilke's line 'you must change your life,' is implicit
in the entire Chekhovian statement (see above), and how it is implicit
in Roth's statement too. The ability to change, however, requires the
ability to take on new roles and perform them credibly; this is something that Kepesh and all of Roth's heroes can do to a greater or lesser
degree. Having lost his talent for performance, however, Axler has
lost the ability to change his life in viable ways; he must summon
all his resources to give one last performance, but at this stage the
Chekhovian imperative requires the most radical change of all.

It might appear difficult to defend Roth for his rather clumsy and
potentially offensive representation of the aging hero's sex with
a lesbian in this book, and it might at first sight seem that Axler's
relationship with a woman twenty-five years his junior constitutes
little more than wish fulfilment for the elderly novelist—certainly
many reviewers took this line. Consider these words from Kathryn
Harrison:

> You don't have to be gay to find such stereotyping offensive. The
> bedroom frolics inspired by something as lurid and ludicrous
> as a green dildo make for embarrassing reading not because of
> the calibre of their sexiness, but because they demean everyone
> involved. Including the reader, who is forced into the position
> of voyeur and thereby made complicit in a vision that doesn't
> allow a lesbian to be anything more than a collection of clichés.
> Representing her sexual orientation—as well as her gender,
> duplicitous daughter of Eve—Pegeen is amoral, capricious and
> cruel. (Unpaginated)

Admittedly the sex scenes are drawn with broad strokes and are
not always convincing in themselves, but the obvious aim is not to

'demean everyone' generally, but to demean the male protagonist specifically, and Pegeen's so-called caprice and cruelty is a requirement
in this sense. The image of a male hero out-performed sexually by
a woman has obvious implications in the broader scheme of Roth's
oeuvre. Roth has a long history of being criticised for constructing
sexist male heroes, of course, so much so that he has gone to rather
elaborate lengths to address such charges both in his interviews, and
in his fiction (a good example being *Deception* as seen above). In *The
Humbling* we have a protagonist who is humiliated by a woman in
a way that, for all its clumsiness and factitiousness, feels more sin-
cere and genuine than when, say, Portnoy is ostensibly humiliated by
Naomi in *Portnoy's Complaint*. As suggested earlier, this is an argument that Portnoy effectively wins and Naomi is the principal figure
of fun. Here it is Axler who is unequivocally the butt of the joke, the
point of which seems to be to reduce and ridicule the male hero. Even
as a breast Kepesh was not as completely unmanned and humiliated
as Axler is here: it will be recalled that in his various sexual activi-
ties with Claire Kepesh retains sexual force, even though his sense
of decorum—or fear of the liminal—won't permit him to request the
extremes he desires ('Fuck on it, Ovington! With your cunt!'). The
comparison is significant. Again the implication is that Kepesh pre-
serves his potency and sexual presence in that book because he never
loses his capacity to perform: as Roth says of him, 'even after he con-
sents to believe that he has actually become a mammary gland, his
mind is alive with alternative ways of being one' (*Reading Myself*,
70). As suggested, Axler is unmanned because he loses this capacity,
and Roth goes to such lengths to humiliate him in order to underscore
this central point about creativity, and the tragedy of losing it: in this
respect the ludicrousness of the sex scenes provides a fitting context
for the character and the extent of his wretchedness.

'What Had to be Done:' Nemesis

Roth's final novel returns us to Newark of the 1940s and focuses on
one of Roth's most earnest and least humorous characters, Bucky
Cantor. Like almost all of Roth's heroes, however, Bucky has a strong

sense of moral obligation. After his mother died in childbirth and his father was convicted of larceny, Bucky was raised by grandparents who paid particular attention to his moral life:

> The grandfather saw to the boy's masculine development, always on the alert to eradicate any weakness that might have been bequeathed—along with poor eyesight—by his natural father and to teach the boy that a man's every endeavour was imbued with responsibility. (*Nemesis*, 22)

Bucky feels the force of that moral responsibility when he is declared unfit for military service in WWII: 'He was ashamed to be seen in civilian clothes' (27), and profoundly guilty for being at home while his friends fight overseas. Instead Bucky spends the summer supervising children in Newark, a task that is itself hazardous given that the city, and Bucky's neighbourhood in particular, is experiencing a devastating polio epidemic. In Greek mythology, Nemesis is the goddess of retribution or vengeance who undermines good fortune, and in this novel it comes in the form of the disease that inexplicably strikes down innocents. By now we are more than familiar with the unfathomable and the catastrophic in Roth's fiction: we have seen how they define the human experience as far as he is concerned. This notion is explored metaphorically in *The Breast* with the inexplicable catastrophe of Kepesh's metamorphosis, and then again and again in stories of people whose life-plans are undermined by nemeses of various kinds: the things that happen 'out of nowhere,' the 'opposing forces,' the 'American berserk,' and 'the omnipotence of caprice.' In *Nemesis* the horror that the latter wreaks comes in the form of the indiscriminate killer polio and reinforces Bucky's sense of a Godless universe: 'I don't know why God created polio in the first place. What was He trying to prove? That we need people on earth who are crippled?' (170).

When Bucky's girlfriend, Marcia, tells him of a job offer at the summer camp where she is working he is faced with a dilemma. His sense of duty tells him that he should stay with the children of Newark, but his heart is drawn to Marcia. The promise of sex with Marcia and the lure of the benign, polio free environment of the rural camp are temptations equal to those faced by any of Roth's conflicted heroes.

'He could take her clothes off, he thought, and see her completely naked. They could be alone on a dark island without their clothes on…On their island he could be far away from everything that was growing harder and harder to bear' (87). Like Kepesh and Everyman, he seems to be a victim of 'the chaos of Eros' as when he capitulates to his desire he is not quite sure how it happened: when he agrees to join Marcia we are told that 'he startled himself…by what he'd just agreed to' (133). Bucky is another character who finds that the inexplicable, unpredictable forces disrupting ordered life come from within as well as without.

While he is wracked with guilt for abandoning his charges in Newark, the summer camp in the mountains of eastern Pennsylvania provides a pastoral idyll reminiscent of those seen before in Roth's writing, not least in the closing scenes of *Professor*. The camp constitutes a 'haven devoid of danger … atop a secluded mountain' (173); and just as Kepesh savoured the days of sex and tranquillity with Claire, so Bucky finds that there's 'something so beguiling about stripping Marcia of her clothes in the dark of an empty island apart from everyone,' and senses the possibility of happiness: 'It's all here! Peace! Love! Health! Beauty! Children! Work! What else was there to do but stay?' (179). But the threat of disaster looms over even the most tranquil moments, suggested partly by Bucky's ambivalence toward his good fortune: 'the happier he felt, the more humiliating it was' (173), and partly by the difficulty he has avoiding arguments with Marcia about her unquestioning belief in God. Disaster eventually strikes when one of Bucky's fellow instructors is stricken with polio, and Bucky suspects himself to be the carrier; subsequently Bucky is also diagnosed with the disease, and it leaves the former athlete handicapped. Bucky refuses to consider the possibility of marrying Marcia—he takes what he considers to be the noble path and shuns her when she visits him, unable to believe that she would want to be stuck 'with a cripple' even though she claimed to be happy to continue their life together. Later when discussing his motivation for the sacrifice he says, 'I did it for her … I did what had to be done' (255).

In the closing sections of the book we discover that this is another Roth story that is mediated by a narratee: Arnold Mesnikoff, who was one of the boys Bucky used to teach during that Newark summer has been telling the story all along. Like Bucky, Arnold contracted polio, but where Bucky retreats from the world—returning to live with his mother and remaining a bachelor—Arnold is married and has made a success of his life. *Nemesis* concludes with Arnold's reminiscences of Bucky teaching the children how to throw the javelin. The 'vigorous and muscular' Bucky threw like Hercules himself and the closing images contrast with the image we now have of the crippled Bucky. Like Kepesh of *The Breast*, then, Bucky is reduced by unfathomable forces and transformed into a diminished version of his former self. Also like Kepesh he strives hard to make sense of his condition: throughout the book Bucky reflects on the nature of a world in which children can die of polio and yet people still believe in God, and in his crippled state this continues. His attempts to find a reason for his suffering, however, merely put him in opposition to a God he doesn't believe in, a rather absurd contradiction identified by Arnold late in the book: the implication of Bucky's antagonism toward the idea of God is godless chaos, 'the tyranny of contingency' which is 'what I believed Mr. Cantor meant when he was decrying what he called God' (243). What Bucky doesn't realise is that his conclusion about Godless chaos renders the whole idea of guilt about this issue meaningless. Bucky's self-flagellation and refusal to marry Marcia is born of guilt, but how can that be a factor here? Polio attacks indiscriminately, but Bucky seems to need to create a meaningful narrative for his life:

> He has to convert tragedy into guilt. He has to find necessity for what happens. There is an epidemic and he needs a reason for it. He has to ask what. Why? Why? That it is pointless, contingent, preposterous, and tragic will not satisfy him. That it is a prolifer-ating virus will not satisfy him. Instead he looks desperately for a deeper cause, this martyr, this maniac of the why. (265)

In *The Breast* Kepesh was also a 'maniac of the why' but, unlike Bucky, he doesn't assume he has an answer: Bucky's inability to allow for brute chance makes him construct a narrative of mean-ing that cripples his thinking in exactly the way polio has crippled his body. In this sense it is significant perhaps that, along with the Swede from *Pastoral*, he is one of the very few Roth protagonists to be explicitly described as humourless; as Arnold tell us, 'He was a largely humourless person … with barely a trace of wit, who never in his life has spoken satirically or with irony, who rarely cracked a joke or spoke in jest' (273). The ability to think humorously or ironically is in part an ability to entertain two concepts simultaneously; it's an ability to entertain incongruity and ambiguity; comedy, in other words, acknowledges that the world occasionally doesn't make sense: as Milan Kundera puts it, comedy 'brutally reveals the meaninglessness of everything' (*The Art of the Novel*, 126). As with the Swede, Bucky's humourlessness parallels his intolerance of incongruity and his inability to reconcile himself to meaninglessness: hence Bucky 'paid a high price in assigning the gravest meaning to his story' (*Nemesis*, 273).

So unlike Arnold, Bucky is unable to change his life, trapped as he is within his specious narrative of guilt, and at first sight he looks like a fool by comparison. However, as is invariably the case with Roth's interrogative books, there is another way to see this. Claudia Roth Pierpont cites J.M. Coetzee's review of the novel as one which made her reassess her initial reading of Bucky as someone suffering from a 'misplaced sense of responsibility' (*Roth Unbound*, 317). According to Coetzee, Bucky is the character who 'takes humanity, and the reach of human understanding, seriously,' and while this may be at odds with his self-interest, he, unlike Arnold, 'keeps an ideal of human dignity alive in the face of fate, Nemesis, the gods, God.' (Coetzee, quoted in *Roth Unbound*, 317). This reading privileges the quest itself, like Roth's early assessment of Kepesh as 'the first heroic character I've ever been able to portray,' Bucky's unwillingness to capitulate to what we might term the indignity of meaninglessness renders him a hero of sorts. The ability to construct ideals and to live by them distinguishes us in the animal kingdom, and Roth's final book makes this point as eloquently as he did in *The Breast*. Bucky is heroic for the same reason Kepesh heroic: he refuses to relinquish his sense of himself as human; he refuses, ultimately, to be abject.

Conclusion

This reading of Roth's canon has shown that recurring themes feature right from the outset of his career. At the deepest level, duty versus desire is his clearest focus. In the early realist work the former is privileged over the latter in stories that seem to endorse social values over individual desires. The comedy *Portnoy's Complaint* tips this hierarchy on its head and celebrates the desiring hero's dissenting voice. The turning point comes in *The Breast*, which we have argued is Roth's first truly interrogative book. In many ways Kepesh is the quintessential Roth hero, and the narrative in which he first appears typifies Roth's approach to the Rothian dilemma from hereon. The books that follow tend to be sophisticated, self-aware reflections on the human condition which are all informed by essentially the same philosophical scepticism and uncertainty. Subsequent Roth heroes can no more fathom their various predicaments than Kepesh can fathom what transformed him into a mammary gland. As a breast Kepesh continues to struggle with the human needs that conflicted him in his former life, and his moral dilemma persists without possibility of resolution. Just as Kepesh cannot find an answer to his problems, nor can any Roth hero to come. The impression that we get in *The Breast* and every post-Kepesh book is that there are no answers. So it can be seen how important this novella is in Roth's development as a writer, and how interesting Kepesh is as a creation. As his story unfolds in *Professor* and *Animal* we find him dealing with the issues that preoccupy Roth as a novelist throughout his career: the problem of self-determination, the relationship between art and life, the tyranny of contingency, and the spectre of mutability and death.

Kepesh is typical of Roth heroes in his need to live his life on his own terms; the latitude to change his life is essential to his sense of wellbeing. Much of Roth's biographical writing suggests that the author shares this trait. Certainly this is the implication of his 1989 memoir, *The Facts: A Novelist's Autobiography*, where he tells of his difficulty finding an environment conducive to a stable life, and appears to be driven by a persistent desire for change. He sounds a little like Portnoy and Messner when he speaks of his need to quit the loving yet stifling home of his parents as a youth, and later after entering a disastrous marriage, he gives an account of his desperation to escape the matrimonial snare that matches Tarnopol's experience in *My Life as a Man*. It appears that Roth in his real life has a history of manoeuvring to avoid or escape entrapments of various kinds. *The Facts* is an experimental memoir in which Roth hands over his so-called unfictionalised life to his characters for comment, and it is worth noting how Zuckerman's remarks on Roth's life would be perfectly applicable to Kepesh's: 'You break out of a series of safe circles...to discover what a life is like 'away' (165). Roth receives a similar response from Maria, Zuckerman's fictional wife:

> As he construes it, the whole thing is a struggle against all those forces inviting him to lose his freedom. Keeping his freedom, giving it away, getting it back—only an American could see the fate of his freedom as the recurring theme of his life. (189)

Roth admits to having commitment issues akin to Kepesh's then, and this adds weight to the notion that Kepesh is close to Roth in terms of his issues and opinions.

Roth in Retirement

At this point there doesn't appear to be a future for Roth as a novelist. Since he announced his retirement after the publication of *Nemesis* he has produced no more stories, and it seems his announcement was in earnest. In his retirement the reading public have had to make do with the various interviews in which he reflects on his reading and on the problems of the modern world. It won't be a surprise that when he does so he sounds exactly like Kepesh. We know that conflict is innate in the self and endemic in society as far as Kepesh is concerned; he sees it in his own character and in the world around him: he is torn by antithetical impulses, of course, and history for him is characterised by warring perspectives vying for the upper hand. As we've seen, this point is stated explicitly in *Animal* when he tells us: 'Argument and counterargument is what history is made of.' This is exactly Roth's view, and he has expressed it in many interviews, most recently in his post-retirement talk with Cynthia Haven, discussing his reading of nineteenth century American history, for instance, he tells us that:

> The questions that preoccupy me at the moment have to do with Bleeding Kansas, Judge Taney and Dred Scott, the Confederacy, the 13th, 14th and 15th amendments, Presidents Johnson and Grant and Reconstruction, the Ku Klux Klan, the Freedman's Bureau, the rise and fall of the Republicans as a moral force and the resurrection of the Democrats, the overcapitalized railroads and the land swindles, the consequences of the Depression of 1873 and 1893, the final driving out of the Indians, American expansionism, land speculation, white Anglo-Saxon racism, Armour and Swift, the Haymarket riot and the making of Chicago, the no-holds-barred triumph of capital, the burgeoning defiance of labor, the great strikes and the violent strikebreakers, the implementation of Jim Crow, the Tilden-Hayes election and the Compromise of 1877, the immigrations from southern and eastern Europe, 320,000 Chinese entering America through San Francisco, women's suffrage, the temperance movement, the Populists, the Progressive reformers. (Unpaginated)

The events he chooses to list, and the manner in which he lists them, is telling: Republicans versus Democrats, the American Indians versus expansionism, triumph of capital versus the great strikes; Reconstruction versus the Ku Klux Klan, and so on. For Roth as for Kepesh, history is conflict.

Kepesh feels that individuals are the unwitting victims of the prevailing ideology; even in a country like America which is free of totalitarianism, people are slaves to convention and specious morality, as he sees with his own son, Kenny, who insists on marrying the woman he impregnates at college, despite Kepesh's protestations. Kepesh invokes the freedoms born of the 60s in order to persuade his son otherwise, but they have no effect in the midst of social expectation. He tells him that 'nobody could make him do what he didn't want to do' (*Animal*, 81) and, again, sounds much like

Roth does in his various assessments of the male condition. In a 2014 interview with Daniel Sandstrom in *The New York Times*, for instance, Roth discusses his various male protagonists, and 'the assailability of vital, tenacious men with their share of peculiarities who are neither mired in weakness nor made of stone and who, almost inevitably, are bowed by blurred moral vision'(unpaginated). Again this could be Kepesh accounting for Kenny's poor life choices, or indeed his own as a younger man.

As a critic Kepesh privileges high art over the ephemeral and the sentimental, of course, and despairs at what he sees as popular culture's capacity to trivialise society, and the unspecified pernicious consequences:

> TV doing what it does best: the triumph of trivialization over tragedy. The triumph of the surface with Barbara Walters. Rather than the destruction of the age old cities an international eruption of the superficial instead. A global outbreak of sentimentality such as even American's hadn't witnessed before. From Sydney to Bethlehem to Times Square the recalculating of clichés occurs at supersonic speeds. No bombs go off no blood is shed, the next bang you hear will be the boom of prosperity and the explosion of markets. Watching this hyped up production of staged pande-monium I have a sense of the moneyed world eagerly entering the prosperous dark ages. A night of human happiness to usher in barbarism.com. To welcome appropriately the shit and the kitsch of the new millennium. A night not to remember but to forget. (*Animal*, 145–6)

Again Kepesh sounds unerringly like Roth here. Speaking again in *The New York Times*, for instance, Roth says,

> The power in any society is with those who get to impose the fantasy. It is no longer, as it was for centuries throughout Europe, the church that imposes its fantasy on the populace, nor is it the totalitarian superstate that imposes the fantasy, as it did for 12 years in Nazi Germany and for 69 years in the Soviet Union. Now the fantasy that prevails is the all-consuming, voraciously consumed popular culture, seemingly spawned by, of all things, freedom. The young especially live according to beliefs that are

thought up for them by the society's most unthinking people and by the businesses least impeded by innocent ends. Ingeniously as their parents and teachers may attempt to protect the young from being drawn, to their detriment, into the moronic amusement park that is now universal, the preponderance of the power is not with them. (Daniel Sandstrom, unpaginated)

The 'moronic amusement park' that Roth identifies in contemporary America is akin to the Kepesh's 'shit and the kitsch of the new millennium.' For both the author and his character, the dark forces of consumerism and big business fuel such developments; just as for Kepesh the 'moneyed world' welcomes 'the prosperous dark ages,' so for Roth it is 'the businesses least impeded by innocent ends' who are set to gain from 'voraciously consumed popular culture.'

A Final Word: Wholeness

Now we can see Roth's writing career in its entirety, it's interesting to reflect on two images that come from the beginning and the end of his writing life. In one of his earliest pieces, published in *Esquire* in 1959, Roth reminisces about boyhood trips to the coast and the image he had of himself whilst playing baseball in front of female spectators. He describes how he would

> Be standing in my bathing suit at the water's edge, tossing a ball back and forth before an audience in which there would be girls...I practised not only throwing but standing, waiting, retrieving. I knew exactly what I wanted to look like, and it was some years after ... that I saw in Florence what I had in mind— it was Michelangelo's David. ('Recollections from Beyond the Last Rope,' 45)

This compares interestingly with the final image we have of Bucky in *Nemesis*: after he's shown lecturing his charges about the classical history of the javelin and the first javelin thrower, 'the giant son of the supreme Greek god, Zeus' (*Nemesis*, 276), Bucky's own body is described in terms suggestive of classical perfection: 'the feet, the legs, the buttocks, the trunk, the arms, the shoulders, even the thick stump of the bull neck—that acting in unison had powered that throw' (279). To Arnold, the narrator, it's this image of the classic male form that had made Bucky look 'invincible' as a younger man. These images of classical physical perfection are suggestive of a desire for wholeness and unity of a kind seen throughout Roth's writing, and it is noteworthy that the author himself should identify so strongly with the classical male form. The search for wholeness in Roth takes various forms, but always exists alongside reflections on masculinity and the implications of being a man. It is significant, of course, that Roth concludes *The Breast* with a reference via Rilke to the Torso of Apollo: this image of a fragmented male suggests that the search for wholeness will remain elusive. We have seen too how the whole idea of maleness is problematic for Roth heroes who constantly perform versions of masculinity: scholar and rake, doctor and pornographer, husband and adulterer, Jewish hero and apostate son, black man and white man, and so on. Roth's men cannot reconcile themselves to a single role: all identities are performances, not least the ones that attempt to unify or encompass multiple identities. We have seen too how elusive certainty is in Roth, and in his representation of men we witness time and again characters who are tormented by doubt, often to the point of psychological disintegration. There is no clearer evidence of this in the whole of Roth's writing than the image of Kepesh as a breast. As Velichka Ivanova says, it is an image that expresses the 'male subject's otherness surfacing in his body,' and it is an eloquent statement that '[m]asculinity is in fact an unstable sign' (42). This instability is at the heart of the Rothian dilemma, and appears to be a creative spur in practically everything that Roth has written. Though his heroes crave wholeness and stability on the one hand, there is a very real sense in which integration and stability is anathema in Roth's novels. We saw, for instance, how Zuckerman depends on his contradictions for his art, but again the clearest expression of this can be seen in Kepesh. Talking of Kepesh in *The Dying Animal*, Ivanova notes that

> When he finally overcomes the despair caused by Consuela's leaving him, he proudly declares: 'My life is untroubled and back in my hands' (123). Ironically, the rest of the story will prove to be yet another assault on his peace of mind. Indeed,

Roth's narrative rebels against the idea of a well-ordered and clearly delineated way of life. The whole book is about 'perpetual *imbalance*' (20). *The Dying Animal* is a catalyst for subversion. (Ivanova, 39)

Ultimately there is a sense in which Kepesh does not want an ordered life, and he doesn't want 'balance;' as with most Roth heroes, it is his desire for wholeness that animates him emotionally and creatively. While the imagined ideal might be a state in which, to quote Kepesh of *The Breast*, 'all is oneself and oneself is all,' it is the desire for such a state, not the realisation of that desire, which fuels both art and life.

Bibliography

Alter, Robert. 'The Education of David Kepesh.' *Partisan Review*, 46 (1979): 478–481.

Anon. 'The Savage Urge.' *The Telegraph*, (30 June, 2001), http://www.telegraph.co.uk/culture/4724378/The-savage-urge.html .

Baker, George. *Realism in Modern Literature*. London: Ungar, 1980.

Bakhtin, Mikhail, *The Dialogic Imagination*. Ed. Michael Holquist; Trans. Caryl Emerson and Michel Holquist. Austin: University of Texas Press, 1981.

Barkham, John, 'Review of *The Professor of Desire*,' *John Barkham Reviews* (October 1st, 1977): 1–2.

Barthes, Roland, *S/Z*. London: Basil Blackwell, 1990.

Bergson, Henri. *Laughter: An Essay on the Meaning of the Comic*. Trans. Cloudesley Brereton and Fred Rothwell. London: Green Integer Books, 1900.

Bersani, Leo, *A Future of Astyanax: Character and Desire in Literature*. Boston: Little Brown and Co., 1976.

Bier, Jesse. 'A Hero at the Breast,' *Carlton Miscellany*, 17 (1979): 214–221.

Bishop, Dorothy. 'Literary Lives…Who Learns from Great Books?' *Ottawa Journal* (November 12th, 1977): unpaginated.

Bloom, Harold. *The Anxiety of Influence: A Theory of Poetry*. Oxford: Oxford University Press, 1973.

Bourjaily, Vance. 'Cool Book on a Warm Topic,' *New York Times Book Review* (September 18th, 1977): 1.

Bradbury, Malcolm and Howard Temperley, eds. *Introduction to American Studies*. London: Longman, 1981.

Bradbury, Malcolm, *The Modern American Novel*. Oxford: Oxford University Press, 1992.

Brady, Charles, 'Roth on Flesh and Spirit.' *Buffalo Evening News* (November 1st, 1977): unpaginated.

Brauner, David, *Philip Roth*. Manchester: Manchester University Press, 2007.

Brent, Jonathan. 'What Facts: A Talk with Roth.' *New York Times Book Review* (September 25th, 1988): 230–236.

Brooker, Peter, ed. *Modernism/Postmodernism*. London: Longman, 1992.

Broyard, Anatole. 'The Voyeur Vu.' *The New York Times* (May 9th, 1981): 13.

Chekhov, Anton. *Eleven Stories*. Trans. Roger Hingley. Oxford: Oxford University Press, 1976.

Cherolis, Stephanie. 'Philip Roth's Pornographic Elegy: *The Dying Animal* as a Contemporary Meditation on Loss.' *Philip Roth Studies*, 2 (Spring 2006): 13–24.

Connor, Stephen. *Postmodernist Culture: An Introduction to Theories of the Contemporary*. London: Blackwell, 1989.

Cowley, Jason. 'The Nihilist.' (Rev. of *The Dying Animal*). *The Atlantic Monthly* (May 2001): 118–20. Online

http://www.theatlantic.com/past/docs/issues/2001/05/cowley.htm

Crews, Frederick. 'Uplift.' *The New York Review of Books* (November 16th, 1972): 18–20.

Dalton-Brown, Sally. 'Is There Life Outside of (the Genre of) the Campus Novel? The Academic Struggles to Find a Place in Today's World.' *The Journal of Popular Culture*, 41.4 (2008): 591–600.

Davidson, Sara. 'Talk with Philip Roth.' *New York Times Book Review* (September 18th, 1977): 9–11.

Dembo, L. S. *The Monological Jew: A Literary Study*. Wisconsin: Wisconsin University Press, 1988.

Eco, Umberto. 'Postmodernism, Irony and the Enjoyable.' *Modernism/Postmodernism*. Ed. Peter Brooker. London: Longman, 1992, 225–228.

Fallowell, Duncan. 'A Suitable Case for Mastectomy.' *Books and Bookmen*, 18 (June, 1973): 70.

Faulkner, Joanne. 'Freud's Concept of the Death Drive and its Relation to the Superego.' *Minerva: an Internet Journal of Philosophy*, 9 (2005): online

http://www.minerva.mic.ul.ie//vol9/Freud.html

Fenninger, Peter. '*The Breast* Needs More Development.' *Charlotte Observer* (October 8th, 1982): unpaginated.

Flood, Alison. 'Judge Withdraws over Philip Roth's Booker Win.' *The Guardian* (May 18th, 2011):

http://www.guardian.co.uk/books/2011/may/18/judge-quits-philip-roth-booker

Freud, Sigmund. 'The Economic Problem of Masochism.' *The Standard Edition of the Complete Psychological Works of Sigmund Freud*, Vol. XIX (1923–25). Ed. and trans. by James Strachey (London: The Hogarth Press, 1961.

——. *Jokes and their Relation to the Unconscious* (1905). London: Penguin, 1991.

Friedman, Melvin. 'Dislocations of Setting and Word: Notes on American Fiction Since 1950.' *Studies in American Fiction*, 5.1 (1977): 79–98.

Gilman, Richard. 'Let's Lynch Lucy.' *New Republic* (June 14th, 1967): 19–20.

Girgus, Sam. 'Between *Goodbye Columbus* and Portnoy: Becoming a Man and a Writer in Roth's Feminist "Family Romance".' *Studies in Jewish American Literature*, 8.2 (1989): 143–153.

Gray, Paul. 'Return of the Jewish Centaur.' *Time* (September 26th, 1977): 78.

Grant, Linda. 'Breast Man.' *The Guardian* (1st June, 2001): http://www.guardian.co.uk/books/2001/jun/30/fiction.philiproth

Greenburg, Martin. *The Terror of Art*. London: Andre Deutsch, 1971.

Goodbar, David. *The Major Phases of Philip Roth*. London: Continuum, 2011.

Harrison, Kathryn. 'Performance Anxiety.' *The New York Times Sunday Book Review* (November 11th 2009):

http://www.nytimes.com/2009/11/15/books/review/Harrison-t.html?pagewanted=all&_r=0

Haven, Cynthia. 'An Interview with Philip Roth: "The Novelist's Obsession Is with Language".' *Stanford University: The Book Haven* (February 3rd, 2014):

http://bookhaven.stanford.edu/2014/02/an-interview-with-philip-roth-the-novelists-obsession-is-with-language/

Hilfer, Tony. *American Fiction Since 1940*. London: Longman, 1992.

Hobbs, Alex. 'Reading the Body in *Philip Roth's American Pastoral*.' *Philip Roth Studies*, 6.1 (Spring, 2010): 69–83, 117.

Howard, Maureen. 'Other Voices.' *Partisan Review*, 35 (1968): 141–152.

Howe, Irving. 'Philip Roth Reconsidered.' *Commentary*, 54.6 (1972): 69–77.

Hutcheon, Linda. *The Poetics of Postmodernism: History, Theory, Fiction*. (London: Routledge, 1998).

Irving, Washington. 'Rural Life in England'. (1819). Collected in *The Sketch Book of Geoffrey Crayon, Gent*. New York: Butler Brothers, 1888, 66–67.

Ivanova, Velichka. 'My Own Foe from the Other Gender: (Mis)representing Women in *The Dying Animal*.' *Philip Roth Studies*, 8.1 (Spring, 2012): 31–44.

Jackson, Rosemary. *Fantasy: The Literature of Subversion*. London: Routledge, 1988.

Jameson, Fredric. 'Imaginary and Symbolic in Lacan: Marxism, Psychoanalytic Criticism, and the Problem of the Subject.' *Yale French Studies*, 55–56 (1977): 338–395.

——. 'Postmodernism and Consumer Society.' In Peter Brooker, ed. *Modernism/Postmodernism*. New York: Longman, 1992, 163–179.

Jones, Judith and Paterson Nance. *Philip Roth*. New York: Ungar, 1981.

Kafka, Franz. 'The Metamorphosis.' *The Collected Stories of Franz Kafka*. Trans. Willa and Edwin Muir. London: Penguin, 1988.

Kaminsky, Alice. 'Philip Roth's Professor Kepesh and the Reality Principle.' *Denver Quarterly*, 13 (1978): 41–54.

Kaprielian, Nelly. 'In Which Philip Roth Announces His Retirement (in English).' *The Paris Review* (November 13th, 2012):

http://www.theparisreview.org/blog/2012/11/13/in-which-philip-roth-announces-his-retirement-in-english/

Kauvar, Elaine M. 'This Doubly Reflected Communication: Roth's "Autobiographies".' *Contemporary Literature*, 36.3 (Autumn, 1995): 412–446.

Kellman, Stephen. 'Reading Himself and Kafka.' *Newsletter of the Kafka Society of America*, 6.1–2 (1982): 25–33.

Keppler, C.F. *The Literature of the Second Self*. Arizona: University of Arizona Press, 1972, 209–210.

Kermode, Frank. *The Sense of an Ending: Studies in the Theory of Fiction*. Oxford: Oxford University Press, 2000.

Kristeva, Julia. *Powers of Horror: An Essay on Abjection*. Trans. Leon S. Roudiez. New York: Columbia University Press, 1982, http://seas3.elte.hu/coursematerial/RuttkayVeronika/Kristeva_-_powers_of_horror.pdf

Kundera, Milan. *The Art of the Novel*. Trans. L. Asher. London: Faber and Faber, 1988.

Lee, Hermione. '"Life Is and": Philip Roth in 1990.' *The Independent on Sunday* (September 2nd, 1990): 12–13.

Levine, Martin. 'Studious by Day, Dissolute by Night.' *Newsday* (September 25th, 1977): 24.

Lyons, Bonnie. 'Jew on the Brain in "Wrathful Philippics".' *Studies in American Jewish Literature*, 8.2 (1989): 186–195.

Mars-Jones, Adam. 'The Sexual License Fee.' *The Observer* (1st July, 2001): http://www.guardian.co.uk/books/2001/jul/01/fiction.philiproth

Marshall, Brenda. *Teaching the Postmodern: Fiction and Theory*. London: Routledge, 1992.

Mathews, Peter. 'The Pornography of Destruction: Performing Annihilation in *The Dying Animal*.' *Philip Roth Studies*, 3.1 (2007): 44–55.

Meisel, Perry. 'Philip Roth's New Novel: Tender is the Knife.' *The Village Voice* (September 12th, 1977): http://perrymeisel.blogspot.co.uk/2010/08/philip-roths-new-novel-tender-is-knife.html

Mepham, John. 'Narratives of Postmodernism.' Edmund Smyth, ed. *Postmodernism and Contemporary Fiction*. London: Batsford, 1991, 138–155.

McDonald, Paul. *Student Guide to Philip Roth*. London: Greenwich Exchange, 2003.

——. *Laughing at the Darkness: Optimism and Postmodernism in American Humour*. Humanities E-Books, 2011.

——. 'American Paleface and Redskin Humour.' *Australian Journal of Comedy*, 5.1 (1999): 7–25.

——. 'The Unmanning Word: Language, Masculinity and Political Correctness in the Writing of David Mamet and Philip Roth.' *Journal of American Studies in Turkey*, 7 (1998): 23–30. http://

www.bilkent.edu.tr/~jast/Number7/Mcdonald.html

——. 'Did You Hear the One About God? Representations of Religion in Post-war Jewish-American Comedy.' Derek Rubin and Hans Krabbendam, eds. *Religion in America: European and American Perspectives*. Amsterdam: Amsterdam University Press, 2004, 155–164.

——. '"They're Trying to Kill Me": Jewish American Humour and The War Against Pop Culture.' *Journal of Popular Culture*, 28.3 (2006): 19–35.

Michel, Pierre. 'Philip Roth's *The Breast*: Reality Adulterated and the Plight of the Writer.' *The Dutch Quarterly Review of Anglo-American Letters*, 5 (1975): 232–239.

——. 'What Price Misanthropy? Philip Roth's Fiction.' *English Studies: A Journal of English Language and Literature*, 58 (1977): 232–239.

Milbauer, Asher Z. and Donald G. Watson, eds. *Reading Philip Roth*. London: Macmillan, 1988.

Mintz, Lawrence E. 'Devil and Angel: Philip Roth's Humour.' *Studies in American Jewish Literature*, 8.2 (1989): 154–167.

Norris, Christopher. *Deconstruction: Theory and Practice*. London: Metheun, 1982.

Parrish, Timothy. 'You Must Change your life: Gender, Desire, and Philip Roth.' (Review of Debra Shostak. *Philip Roth: Countertexts, Counterlives*.) *Twentieth Century Literature*, 52.4 (Winter, 2006): 482–488.

——. 'Roth and Ethnic Identity.' Timothy Parrish, ed. *The Cambridge Companion to Philip Roth*. Cambridge: Cambridge University Press, 2007, 127–142.

Piette, Alain. 'The Devil's Advocate: David Mamet's *Oleanna* and Political Correctness.' Marc Maufort, ed. *Staging Difference: Cultural Pluralism in American Theatre and Drama*. New York: Peter Lang, 1995.

Pinsker, Sanford, ed. *Critical Essays on Philip Roth*. Boston: G.K Hall, 1982.

Posnock, Ross. *Philip Roth's Rude Truth: The Art of Immaturity*. Princeton: Princeton University Press, 2006.

Pye, Gillian. 'Comedy Theory and Postmodernism.' *Humor*, 19.1 (2006): 53–70.

Quartz, B.K. 'The Rapacity of One Nearly Buried Alive.' *Massachusetts Review*, 24 (1983): 590–608.

Raban, Jonathan. 'Bad Language.' *Encounter* (December, 1973): 76–80.

Rahv, Philp. 'Paleface and Redskin.' Philip Rahv. *Literature and the Sixth Sense*. London: Faber and Faber, 1970, 1–7.

———. 'The Education of Anton Chekhov.' Philip Rahv. *Literature and the Sixth Sense*. London: Faber and Faber, 1970, 216–222.

Riesman, David, with Nathan Glazer and Reuel Denney. *The Lonely Crown: A Study of the Changing American Character*. (1950). Yale: Yale University Press, 1969.

Rogers, Bernard, F. *Philip Roth*. Boston: Twayne, 1978.

Rosenfield, Claire. 'The Shadow Within: The Conscious and the Unconscious Use of the Double.' *Daedalus*, 92 (Spring, 1963): 326–344.

Ross, Andrew, ed. *Universal Abandon? The Politics of Postmodernism*. Minnesota: University of Minnesota Press, 1988.

Roth Pierpont, Claudia. *Roth Unbound: A Writer and His Books*. London, Jonathan Cape, 2014.

Roth, Richard. 'Roth's Best Novel Yet.' *The Weekly Reader* (October 5th, 1977): 17.

Roth, Philip. *Goodbye Columbus*. Boston: Houghton Mifflin, 1959.

———. 'Recollections from Beyond the Last Rope.' *Harper's Magazine* (July 1959): 42–48.

——. 'Letters from Readers.' *Commentary* (September, 1961): 248–252.

——. *Letting Go*. New York: Random House, 1962.

——. *When She Was Good*. Jonathan Cape, 1967.

——. *Portnoy's Complaint*. London: Jonathan Cape Ltd, 1971.

——. *Reading Myself and Others*. London: Penguin, 1985.

——. *The Breast*. New York: Holt, Rinehart and Winston, 1972.

——. *The Breast*. London: Vintage, 2006.

——. *My Life as a Man*. London: Jonathan Cape, 1974.

——. *The Professor of Desire*. (1977). London: Jonathan Cape, 1978.

——. *The Counterlife*. New York: Farrar, 1987.

——. *The Facts*. London: Jonathan Cape, 1989.

——. *Operation Shylock*. London: Jonathan Cape, 1993.

——. *Sabbath's Theater*. London: Random House, 1995.

——. *American Pastoral*. London: Jonathan Cape, 1997.

——. *I Married a Communist*. London: Jonathan Cape, 1998.

——. *The Human Stain*. London: Jonathan Cape, 2000.

——. *Zuckerman Bound: The Ghost Writer, Zuckerman Unbound, The Anatomy Lesson, The Prague Orgy*. New York: Farrar, Straus, Giroux, 1985. *The Ghost Writer* first published 1979, *Zuckerman Unbound* first published 1981, *The Anatomy Lesson* first published 1983, *The Prague Orgy* first published, 1985.

——. *The Plot Against America*. London: Jonathan Cape, 2004.

——. *The Dying Animal*. London: Vintage, 2006.

——. *Everyman*. London, Jonathan Cape, 2006.

——. *Exit Ghost*. London: Jonathan Cape, 2007.

——. *Indignation*. London: Vintage, 2009.

——. *The Humbling*. London: Jonathan Cape, 2009.

——. *Nemesis*. London: Vintage, 2011.

Roth, Zoe. 'Against Representation: Death, Desire, and Art in Philip Roth's *The Dying Animal*.' *Philip Roth Studies* (Spring, 2012): 95–100.

Royal, Derek Parker. 'Pastoral Dreams and National Identity.' Derek Parker Royal, ed. *Philip Roth: New Perspectives on an American Author*. Westport, CT: Praeger, 2005, 185–209.

Rushdie, Salman. 'Is Nothing Sacred?' Salman Rushdie. *Imaginary Homelands: Essays and Criticism 1981–1991*. Cambridge: Granta, 1991, 415–429.

Sabiston, Elisabeth. 'A New Fable for Critics: Philip Roth's *The Breast*.' *International Fiction Review*, 2 (1975): 27–34.

Safer, Elaine. *Mocking the Age: The Later Novels of Philip Roth*. Albany State: University of New York Press, 2006.

Samuels, Charles. 'The Part that Sam Levenson Leaves Out.' *Chicago Tribune Book World* (February 16th, 1969): 1.

Sandstrom, Daniel. 'My Life as a Writer.' *The New York Times* (March, 2nd, 2014): http://www.nytimes.com/2014/03/16/books/review/my-life-as-a-writer.html?_r=0

Scott, A. O. 'Alter Alter Ego: Philip Roth Brings Back David Kepesh, Formerly a Breast.' *New York Times Online* (May 27th, 2001): http://www.nytimes.com/books/01/05/27/reviews/010527.27scottt.html)

Scott, Robert F. 'It's a Small World, after All: Assessing the Contemporary Campus Novel.' *The Journal of the Midwest Modern Language Association*, 37.1 (Spring, 2004): 81–87.

Shepherd, R.Z. 'Braless in Gaza.' *Time* (September 25th, 1972): 94–98.

Shipe, Matthew. '*Exit Ghost* and the Politics of Late Style.' *Philip Roth Studies*, 5.2 (2009): 189–204.

Shostak, Debra. 'Roth and Gender.' Timothy Parrish, ed. *The Cambridge Companion to Philip Roth*. Cambridge: Cambridge University Press, 2007, 110–146.

——*Philip Roth: Countertexts, Counterlives*. Columbia, SC: University of South Carolina Press, 2004.

Sinclair, Clive. 'The Son is the Father of the Man.' Asher Z. Milbauer and Donald G. Watson, eds. *Reading Philip Roth*. London: Macmillan, 1988, 168–179.

Siegel, Ben. 'The Myths of Summer: Philip Roth's *The Great American Novel*.' *Contemporary Literature*, 17 (1976): 189–196.

Siegel, Jason. '*The Plot Against America*: Philip Roth's Counter-Plot to American History.' *MELUS*, 37.1 (2012): 131–154.

Simonburg, Larry. 'Roth Referees a Fight.' *Boston Phoenix* (November 22nd, 1977): unpaginated.

Smyth, Edmund, ed. *Postmodernism and Contemporary Fiction*. London: Batsford, 1991.

Snowman, Daniel. 'The Sixties and Seventies.' Malcolm Bradbury and Howard Temperley, eds. *Introduction to American Studies*. London: Longman, 1981, 276–295.

Solotaroff, Ted. 'Fiction.' *Esquire* (October, 1972): 178.

Sontag, Susan. 'Against Interpretation.' in David Lodge, ed. *Twentieth Century Literary Criticism*. London: Longman, 652–660.

Stephenson, David. 'The Activists.' *Daedalus*, 92 (1963): 238–249.

Swingewood, Alan. *Sociological Poetics and Aesthetic Theory*. London: Macmillan, 1986.

Tanner, Tony. *Scenes of Nature, Signs of Men: Essays on 19th and 20th Century American Literature*. Cambridge: Cambridge University Press, 1987.

Thorlby, Anthony. *Kafka: A Study*. London: Heinemann, 1972.

Towers, Robert. 'One Man Band.' *New York Review of Books* (October 27th, 1977): 12–14.

Todorov, Tzvetan. *The Fantastic: A Structural Approach to a Literary Genre*. Trans. Richard Howard. Cleveland: Case Western Reserve University Press, 1973.

Trendel, Aristie. 'Master and Pupil in Philip Roth's *The Dying Animal*.' *Philip Roth Studies*, 3.1 (2007): 56–65.

Updike, John. 'Yahweh Over Dionysus, in Disputed Decision.' *The New Yorker* (November 7th, 1983): PAGE.

——. 'Wrestling to be Born.' *The New Yorker* (March, 1987): 107–108.

Varvogli, Aliki. 'The Inscription of Terrorism: Philip Roth's American Pastoral.' *Philip Roth Studies*, 3.2 (Fall 2007): 101–111.

Wade, Stephen. *The Imagination in Transit: The Fiction of Philip Roth*. Sheffield: Sheffield Academic Press, 1996.

West, Kevin R., 'Professing Desire: The Kepesh Novels', in Derek Parker Royal, ed. *Philip Roth: New Perspectives on an American Author*. London: Praeger, 2005, 225–237.

Wirth-Nesher, Hannah. 'Roth's Autobiographical Writings.' Timothy Parrish, ed. *The Cambridge Companion to Philip Roth*. Cambridge: Cambridge University Press, 2007, 158–173.

Woolf, Geoffrey. 'A Novel with Compassion.' *Washington Post* (June 15th, 1967): Unpaginated.

Yaross Lee, Judith. 'Affairs of the Breast: Philip Roth and David Kepesh.' Ben Siegel and Jay. L. Halio, eds. *Playful and Serious: Philip Roth as a Comic Writer*. Newark: University of Delaware Press, 2010, 68–91.

Yeats, W. B. 'Sailing to Byzantium.' *Collected Poems of W.B Yeats*. Ed. Richard J. Finneran. New York: Macmillan, 1984, 204.

A Note on the Authors

Paul McDonald works at the University of Wolverhampton where he is Senior Lecturer in American Literature, and Course Leader for Creative Writing. He is the author of fifteen books including poetry, fiction, and criticism. Among his other HEB titles are, *Laughing at the Darkness* (2010), *The Philosophy of Humour* (2012), and *Reading 'Beloved'* (2014). He has a keen interest in ancient humour, and takes perverse pleasure in the fact that Googling 'the oldest joke in the world' generates several hundred pages with his name on.

Samantha Roden is a Lead Practitioner for English at NEW Academy (North East Wolverhampton). She writes educational resources, digital pedagogical guides and conducts national webinars for Cambridge University Press. Her research interests include teaching writing through drama, and she has conducted workshops on this topic in numerous contexts, including the University of Wolverhampton. Her poetry has appeared in several journals and her first full collection, *Catch Ourselves in Glass*, is forthcoming.

Contemporary American Literature

General Editors :
Chris Gair (Glasgow) & Aliki Varvogli (Dundee)

The editors invite proposals for e-books to be included in this series of approaches to American literature since 1970. We seek typescripts and proposals for books in any of the following (or similar) areas:

- Genre or theme-based studies of contemporary American writing (e.g. immigration and/or emigration narratives, new journalism, neo-slave narratives, travel writing, the short story, crime fiction, science fiction and fantasy writing)
- Theoretical studies of contemporary American literature (e.g. approaches based on gender studies, circum-Atlanticism, environmentalism, postmodernism, race, ethnicity, class)
- Critical studies of significant novelists, poets, dramatists, and other artists in relation to contemporary American culture

Titles published to date:

Paul McDonald, *Laughing at the Darkness: Postmodernism and Optimism in American Humour*

Reinaldo Francisco Silva, *Portuguese American Literature*

John Tanner, *Landscapes of Language: The Achievement and Context of Richard Brautigan's Fiction*

Humanities-Ebooks.co.uk

All Humanities Ebooks titles are available to Libraries through EBL, Ebrary and EBSCO

Some Academic titles

Sibylle Baumbach, *Shakespeare and the Art of Physiognomy**
John Beer, *Blake's Humanism*
John Beer, *The Achievement of E M Forster*
Jared Curtis, ed., *The Fenwick Notes of William Wordsworth**
Steven Duncan, *Analytic Philosophy of Religion: its History since 1955**
Richard Gravil, *William Wordsworth and Helen Maria Williams; or, the Perils of Sensibility**
John K Hale, *Milton as Multilingual: Selected Essays 1982–2004*
Simon Hull, ed., *The British Periodical Text, 1797–1835*
Rob Johnson, Mark Levene and Penny Roberts, eds., *History at the End of the World**
John Lennard, *Modern Dragons and other Essays on Genre Fiction**
Paul McDonald, *Laughing at the Darkness* *
C W R D Moseley, *Shakespeare's History Plays*
Colin Nicholson, *Fivefathers: Interviews with late Twentieth-Century Scottish Poets*
Keith Sagar, *D. H. Lawrence: Poet**
Reinaldo Francisco Silva, *Portuguese American Literature**
John Tanner, *Landscapes of Language: The Achievement and Context of Richard Brautigan's Fiction**
Trudi Tate, *Modernism, History and the First World War**
William Wordsworth, *Concerning the Convention of Cintra**
W J B Owen and J W Smyser, eds., *Wordsworth's Political Writings**
The Poems of William Wordsworth: Collected Reading Texts from the Cornell Wordsworth, 3 vols.*

* These titles are also available in paperback using links from
http://www.humanities-ebooks.co.uk

www.ingramcontent.com/pod-product-compliance
Lightning Source LLC
Chambersburg PA
CBHW021057090426
42738CB00006B/387